BREAI

MW01098726

By
Hal G. Hannon

ACKNOWLEDGEMENTS

I thank
Madam Justice Susan Griffin and all you haters out there whose enmity gave birth to the concept of this book.

I also thank
my friends Dave, Donovan, Harvey, Jonathan, and Sarah whose encouragement helped make that concept real, as well as my friends from the street whose plight tempered my anger and touched my heart, making some words spill onto the pages.

Lastly, I thank
my roommate for her selfless concern for her friends from the street which allowed her to give me permission to make a part of her journey so public by publishing this book.

DEDICATION

This book is dedicated to the women who find the courage no longer to tolerate abuse, and instead call the police to protect them.

These women are my heroes and every one of them has the chance to be a hero to her family and to herself by shedding her abuser.

May God bless them in their struggle to break free from their abusers and give them the strength to rise up against them and regain their self respect and their lives.

FORWARD

To those who physically, emotionally, or sexually abuse children, the opening poem, the violence, the lost souls, the death of the young girl in Chapter 1, along with many other such deaths, and the circumstances and addicts detailed in this book are your legacy. May you be dragged to hell, screaming for mercy, and receive none.

To those who have yet to try drugs, I hope that you will end your curiosity through this vicarious trip into the reality of this dark and frightenedly sinister world.

To those who are hardcore drug users, despair, prison, and death await you unless you get the help you need to quit. There is a road out and it starts with learning how to love and respect yourself.

To those who are casual users, you might think that you are in control, but you are not. The drugs are in control; that is why they call it "being under the influence."

To those who think you are too smart ever to get addicted, they don't call it "dope" because it makes you smart.

To those who are curious about the drug culture, read and sate your curiosity, then resolve to do everything you can to ensure that you and those whom you love never become part of a book such as this.

Author's Note: This book was written for all of you, no matter where you live, because while the major cities may already be lost, what is in this book is now part of a siege on smaller, urban areas throughout North America.

PREFACE

The Monster Deep Inside[1]

If all the world could only see
all the problems that seem to gather
and the tears that fall but don't really matter,
the creature that eats up all of me,
the monster that is so deep inside,
the one I deeply want to hide.
It is a seed that was planted long ago,
a part of me I don't want to show,
It rips all of my life apart.
It makes me look like I have no heart.
It makes me look like something I'm not.
It shows what I have not been taught.
It twists and turns, hurts and burns.
The monster shows I have no concerns.

[1]A poem written by an anonymous drug addicted prostitute and gifted to the author

THE ONLY ABSOLUTE RESPECT
IS ABSOLUTE TRUTH.

SECTION ONE

Orlando Gibbons: "The silver swan, who, living had no note, when death approach'd unlocked her silent throat..."

CHAPTER 1

IT'S ALRIGHT TO CRY

Unknown Author: **"Some say you are too painful to remember. I say you are too precious to forget!"**

Today is May 17, 2014, and I was just told of the death of a young lady yesterday. She was a physically beautiful girl, but that is not the point; it wouldn't be any different had she been physically ugly.

From the few brief times during which we had spoken with one another, she had also radiated an inner beauty, but again, that is not the point either. The point is she was only fifteen years old and she is dead.

Just last week I had seen her sitting on a grassy slope as I drove by. She was near one of the homeless shelters with a few of her friends, whom I did not know, and I gave her a bowl of fresh strawberries, a minor kindness for which I was rewarded with a major smile that almost overshadowed her twinkling, "*Thank you.*"

Her sincere reaction made me feel as though there existed a sea of beauty in the world of ugliness that surrounded her life.

As I write these words, oceans of rage are rolling down my cheeks and anger is demanding a way out of my soul. You see, this child of God never had a chance at life, and as the person who told me of her death said, "*Now she will finally have the peace a child deserves.*"

Purportedly, she was the daughter of two addicts. When the parents split apart, her mother's new boyfriend, according to her, sexually molested her, while her real father roamed the streets, playing tough guy and using and slinging his dope.

The story has it that some nameless, shameless, but never blameless thirtyish year old debauchee with kids of his own, well known for his violence and depravities, was actually sexually defiling this young lady on a regular basis and that this soulless degenerate gave her enough heroin to overdose.

Whether he overdosed her by design or by accident might never be known but for his sick sexual behavior, I pray that this slime dies as a eunuch, slowly, alone, and shaking in fear and that he spends eternity in the hands of Torquemada and may that grand inquisitor torture this repulsive pedophile for the truth, but never believe a single word out of his mouth.

Do not let it get lost on you that a child who may have someday been a mother, or any of a number of other noble things, is now with the angels and only a memory and a loss to us.

Do any of you people get it yet; is anybody out there listening? We now grieve another innocent. This is where child abuse leads; this is where drugs lead.

Stop with the fucking abuses; stop with the fucking excuses; and stop with the fucking drugs. Just stop, I beg you; just fucking stop.

CHAPTER 2

SWING LOW SWEET CHARIOT

Khalil Gibran: "The wolves prey upon the lambs in the darkness of the night, but the blood stains remain upon the stones in the valley until the dawn comes, and the sun reveals the crime to all."

It was 8:30 a.m. on April 9, 2009, and the first strand of the morning sun was cutting through the gap in the flimsy drape covering his sliding patio door, slicing the air with a rivulet of light filled with dancing dust mites, and casting a beam of brightness on his pillow.

He covered his eyes trying to shield himself from the sun's awakening effect. He hadn't had enough time away from life's pressures; he needed to escape longer.

When it comes to temporarily escaping realities that have become too unbearable to face, there is little difference between dope and sleep; and one instinctively seizes the nearest escape. At this moment, sleep was closest at hand, so it was his magic carpet of choice.

He groaned, rolled over trying harder to block the offending light, tugged the pillow tighter atop his head, and wished for more darkness so he could resume his dreams and avoid another day of thinking about things that tortured his mind.

He didn't remember what time he had gone to bed last night and only gave the thought a fleeting recognition. His body was starved for sleep, for water and for food, but sleep was making the biggest demand on him and was also the most expedient. He pulled the pillow even tighter to his head and pushed himself harder into the mattress.

Three hours later he felt as though he had just dozed off and looked at the clock twice to make sure he was reading the correct time.

Then it hit him; there had been several people here last night; images of twenty dollar bills and twenty dollar rocks flashed through his mind. He vaguely remembered the last guy leaving, pulling the apartment door closed behind him.

He also remembered that today was payday. It was time for money and money could help him temporarily chase away his demons again. That thought started an almost reflexive chain reaction; he hurriedly got dressed, splashed some water on his face, and rushed out of the apartment. He then picked up his pay cheque, cashed it, met a dealer, scored some dope and went home to relax and escape.

Sometime after 8:00 p.m. there came a rudely loud knock at the door. Paul crossed the few steps from his couch to the locked entry door that opened to the hallway. Upon opening the door, a blonde-headed male rushed past him as the two other men at the doorway looked on in surprise at what was happening.

Putting Paul in a police choke hold from behind, the blonde assailant dragged Paul to the floor, with both him and Paul on their back. Paul struggled to break the hold and as he fought his pant bottoms rode up on his ankles, exposing the wad of cash secreted in his socks.

The other two grabbed the money and bolted out the door. The assailant, seeing that the money was headed toward the hallway, pulled himself out from underneath Paul, rising to his feet, and Paul started screaming and trying to grab his attacker's legs. Some of the money they took was money Paul had set aside to give to his family and Paul wanted to attract attention to the fact that he was being robbed.

Paul's attacker, anxiously and angrily realizing that Paul's screaming would attract unwanted attention and already having enough troubles with the law for other crimes, turned back to Paul who was still on back and pushed Paul down with his hands as he sat on Paul's chest so that Paul could not get up, and began strangling Paul with his two hands around Paul's neck.

Paul was losing the fight; the devil at his throat kept squeezing; Paul could feel his knees weakening and could no longer resist the unrelenting pressure. His heart was pounding now. He screamed out, *"Help me, somebody help me please."*

He didn't know if a voice had actually come from his larynx or if the scream was only in his mind. He was scared, more scared than he had ever been in his life.

The other two had fled with his money; *"Was it a minute ago or an hour ago?"* He didn't know. He wondered why this devil was still choking him when he had no money.

Paul was still on his back, but this time with his attacker weight holding him to the floor. Their faces were only inches apart now as Paul looked into the eyes of a killer and the killer looked into Paul's eyes to see Paul's desperation and fear.

Paul flailed at his assailant's arms, trying desperately to break the death grip. He thrust his hands at the attacker's face trying to gouge at his attacker's eyes, but the killer stretched his neck upward, pulling his chin in the air and his head back as he bit at Paul's fingers.

Nothing was working; Paul was losing strength with each movement. Even his mind was finding it difficult to fully engage his enemy as his willpower to survive was weakening; he couldn't decide whether to continue to fight, or not; it seemed almost easier to quit than to continue.

He needed his brain to focus, but he sensed the end though and thought, "*So this is how I die.*" He wondered, "*Why won't my body fight, why?*"

He begged himself for strength, tried frantically to will the power back into his arms, tried to command his legs to give one last thrust, and gave another burning gasp for air, but the terror he felt was becoming a peaceful terror because every effort he could muster was failing.

Memories of his family raced through his mind in a slow-motion pictographic display, like the drawings youngsters would make and flip through to give a sense of motion to stick figures. He saw images of his childhood in a misty background, saw a bright flash of light, and then his brain exploded into a black nothingness and suddenly it didn't matter anymore.

Paul was dead, murdered without mercy and he hadn't even known why. He didn't feel the indignity of his body being dragged to the closet and clumsily stuffed halfway in with his feet pointing accusingly at his killer, or see Wyatt Evan Prince exit the suite and slink off into the hallway to savor the evil he had committed.

I have seen the same Angels beckoning me that Paul saw, felt the same fear, seen my life flash before me, and grappled with an enemy I could not control, so I know what Paul felt and I have more compassion for him that you can imagine.

The difference is that my assailant was a blockage in my coronary artery and a doctor brought me back to life. Paul was not as lucky because his assailant was a vicious, blonde-haired fiend who did not want to save him, but only wanted to kill him.

CHAPTER 3

THE FAT LADY SINGS

Dope is the devil and destroys all things that are valuable: family, justice, honesty and honor.

When you do dope as an intrinsic part of your life, there is nothing either black or white. Everything good has its downside and every punishment, even pain, can have an upside.

Roy Clark: "Yesterday when I was young there were so many songs that needed to be sung..."

It was 12:30 a.m. on a Sunday, spring morning and a prostitute was just approaching the apartment complex. It was an old building, built twenty-two years ago by builders who had hopes of retired people and families living there, of children playing in the park across the street, and of the aroma of home cooked meals wafting down its corridors.

Such hopes were gone now though; the families had been driven away by crime and drugs, despite the fact that an elementary school was only a scant four blocks to the west. The older, retired pensioners had long since abandoned the building to look for residences wherein they felt safe.

During the daylight hours, the park still had the fresh smell of recently mown grass. Its benches were stone, but yet somehow soft and inviting.

Perhaps it was the view of the granite mountains looming large in the background that made them so, at least by comparison, or perhaps it was the communal garden that sat beside the playground and invited all who had the inclination and the energy to grow produce for their own personal consumption. Or maybe it was the sand filled play plot waiting for children to bounce and laugh.

While most things are hidden by the dark, it was daylight that hid the evil just across the street and the reason why this pristine and inviting little park was so lifeless.

On any sunny summer afternoon, sitting in the park and looking back at the apartment complex across the street, things looked almost peaceful. The only signs that something was not quite right were the total absence of children entering the building and the always slightly open curtain in the basement window behind which resided a pair of eyes constantly scanning the street for any sign of the police.

However, this was Sunday morning at 12:30 a.m. and there was no sunlight, only darkness. So the broken lives, shattered dreams, and missing innocence were on open display.

On this particular Sunday morning, the prostitute had just broken (scored a paying date) and she was headed to Doc's (not his real name) to enjoy the rewards of her labor. It had taken a scant fifteen minutes standing at the corner before a john in a metallic blue Nissan Sentra caught her nod and quickly pulled over to invite her into his car.

Normally she charged forty for a blow job, sixty for a lay, and eighty for half and half, but this was her first date of the evening and she was anxious to get her night started right by getting an early twenty rock, so the john was able to negotiate a $20.00 blow job and the prostitute was about to have her first hoot (smoke of crack) of the night.

As she approached the back entrance to the apartment building, the peering eyes behind the half-cocked curtain recognized her and a quick signal was given to the doorman that all was okay. She opened the now unlocked side door of the apartment complex and followed Isaac (not his real name) the few steps down the musty hallway toward the second apartment on the right.

Isaac was a thirty-seven year old ex-computer programmer who looked as though he lived his life in a dumpster that never had food thrown in it. His light brown, curly hair was uneven and hanging close to his neck. It was apparent that his full length, scraggly beard was more a product of not shaving than a product of intent.

His clothes bore huge creases that used to be wrinkles and you could almost match the dirt on them to that which crusted on his face and seemed to grow from his beard. Isaac was Doc's doorman and Doc pieced him off with a ten rock several times an evening in return for his services.

That wasn't much for pay, but it was in keeping with Isaac's inability to earn money with which to supply his dope habit. If it wasn't for Doc, Isaac's addiction would have long ago driven him into an armed robbery or worse. Doc kept him out of jail and Isaac knew it.

The problems for Isaac were that he was not female and therefore has nothing to sell, that his looks forbid him being an effective con artist, that those same looks gave him a suspicious appearance making it almost impossible for him to go into residential neighborhoods looking for the correct houses to burgle, and that there wasn't a high demand for computer programmers in the drug corridors and crack shacks of the world. So, he had to support his habit by being useful to Doc and other dealers and by begging for handouts on the street.

Isaac opened the apartment door for the prostitute and she stepped into a short and narrow hallway leading past a bathroom to the kitchen. Off the center of the left wall of the kitchen was a door to the living room, looking into the living room there was a single bedroom door on the back wall directly opposite the door from the kitchen. Each room had a double sliding window that overlooked the park across the street; well, more like under-looked it; this was a basement apartment starving for natural light.

The apartment carpet was an ugly yellow shag with years of use and abuse having worn and stained it to a state of patchiness and filth. The furniture was sparse, Spartan, and shoddy.

In the kitchen, there was a brown, wooden table crammed against the wall to keep it from falling on one of its three unstable legs. The kitchen counter was strewn with two week old food and the sink filled with trash.

There was a large fish bowl filled with used rigs (hypodermic needles), most with their orange caps on to protect against an accidental poke, but some uncapped as if a warning from the users that your health was not their concern. The stench of urine emanating from the almost un-flushable toilet in hallway bathroom overpowered the stale, smoke filled air.

In the living room, an uncovered, double bed mattress lay on the floor, crammed into the corner to the left on the opposite wall from the entry. Passing through the living room and entering the bedroom, sitting on a telephone stand underneath the window and against the right hand wall, there was a thirteen inch black and white television with a coat hanger for an antenna.

Directly ahead, opposite the door, was an old Spanish-style couch, avocado green, with its cushions frayed, its springs sagging, and its foam squeezing out from its frayed seams like a hernia through the wall of a muscle. Beside the couch, on the opposite wall from the television, sitting on a TV stand, was a small, simple, modern microwave oven. This was the most precious and powerful device in the apartment.

Within seconds, it cooks dreams and sends people scurrying for money. It has the power to force a sixteen year old girl to sell her body, to coerce a mother into abandoning her children, to convince a man to break into a house or store, to have teenagers and adults steal from their grandparents, and to control the lives of everyone who entered this apartment.

By simply adding a little baking soda and water and twisting a knob, this little device turns powdered cocaine into rock cocaine, a substance as expensive as gold and more sought after by addicts than their mother's love.

Sitting on the floor leaning against the front of the couch, was Harold "Doc" Jones. Doc was just rolling a precious white blob onto the coffee table behind which he squatted. The room was alive with anticipation. Twenty dollar bills were being thrown on the coffee table as Doc began cutting little white rocks from the marble. He would soon need more cocaine.

In a normal business, the boss would never handle such mundane chores as re-supplying. Instead, he would assign that duty to a trusted employee or friend, but this was not a normal business. This was the drug business. Years of using, conning, dealing, and stealing had taught Doc that when it came to dope there was nobody you could trust, not even your mother or your brother. Doc wasn't worried about sending someone out with the money. He knew the money would actually get spent on dope.

What worried him was whether or not the dope would make it back. It's the first rule of the street, money always finds dope, and dope always finds money. Unfortunately, there is no rule that the dope finds it way back to the real buyer. So, Doc would have to go himself.

The prostitute melted half of her rock onto the brillo which was pushed slightly back into one end of the clear glass tube that was both her pipe and her instrument of pleasure. As she applied a steady flame to the melted white glob, she inhaled deeply from the other end, holding her breath for as long as possible before exhaling. The longer she could hold in the smoke and the deeper that she could inhale it, the stronger the high would be.

Exhaling, she placed the other half of her rock on the end of her pipe. As she finished melting the second half of her precious rock, she heard the sound of the apartment door crashing in and a cop's voice yelling, "*This is the police; everybody stay where you are and get down on the floor.*"

Half the people in the room had already hit the floor before hearing the order, but Doc just sat there wondering how in the hell you could stay where you are and hit the floor at the same time. Everybody in the apartment had been through this many times in the past and the sound of the crashing door made their trip to the floor a Pavlovian response for most of them.

The prostitute proceeded to burn her toke and get it inhaled as quickly as possible. She wasn't trying to hide the evidence, but rather to not waste a good rock just because six (street name for the police) chose this moment to bust in. She was angry, not because she would now have to deal with the police, but because this kind of thing always ruins a good high. She had given that asshole in the blue Sentra a blow job and she wanted her high, especially since the old bastard took fifteen minutes to cum and made her listen to him talk dirty.

Charging into the room, grabbing her by the back of her collar and pulling her to the floor, a cop screamed, "*I told you to get down.*" Now, just what she feared would happen had happened; he had ruined her high. She said to herself, "*God I hate the fucking cops, and especially this prick.*"

Doc was sitting on the floor trying to secret his money under the couch when a police boot caught him on his right temple, blurring his vision and sending pain messages to his brain. In a single motion, the cop reached down to grab the cash with one hand while his other hand extracted the handcuffs from their black holster on the left side of his belt. Laying the cash on the table, he quickly cuffed Doc, and lifting him upright by his cuffed wrists, threw him onto the couch telling him to keep quiet and not to move, and the next time to keep his hands where they could be seen, that there could have been a gun under the couch.

"*Whose dope is this on the table?*" The responses were stillborn. "*Well Doc, it must be yours; it was sitting right in front of you and this is your apartment,*" the cop said. "*Not mine,*" responded Doc.

One of the female cops was blond, in her mid twenties, 5' 9" tall, weighing approximately 150 pounds, and would have been called "pretty" by the street if they didn't already call her "The Bitch." It was a nickname she wore with pride. Her specialty was trying to convince the male pushers and users that she was as tough as they were and trying to intimidate street prostitutes into believing she was tougher.

The truth was though, that despite all her bravado, she created no fear in the men, only contempt. Most of them wanted to rape her, not because they bore any real sexual desire for her, but because it would humiliate and terrorize her. The girls wanted to watch them do it.

She created no fear in the girls either; all of them had already been beaten multiple times by their male relatives, husbands, or lovers and nothing The Bitch could do or say would ever approach the pain of those beatings. The only thing that came close to a fear was that they might get thrown in jail overnight and miss a few dates, and with that, the ability to buy drugs.

But even this was not a fear; it was more of a mixed blessing in their minds. For some it would mean that the high they would get from their dope when they got out would be even more powerful because of its absence from their bodies. Coming off heroin is called kicking because as the heroin leaches out of the bones during withdrawal, the addict involuntarily kicks their legs to deal with the discomfort and pain.

For others it would mean an opportunity to think again about getting clean, something they had been meaning to think more about for the past two years. And for still others it would mean that they could sleep for twelve hours because they had been awake for the last two or three days. For many though, it would mean that they would wake up in the morning needing heroin before they became violently ill from withdrawal symptoms.

This was no fear though; it was a reality to which they had become hardened. Each of these people had been through this routine as seldom as once a month and as often as twice a week, and those numbers do not reflect the times that the boys in blue had jacked them up on the street, searching them, breaking their paraphernalia, taking their money, and making them listen to a ten minute lecture.

That had happened multiple times in a single day to some of them. This was business as usual to them and something to be endured, something that went with the territory, a price to be paid over and above the actual monetary costs of their habits.

Of course, they rarely thought about those other than monetary costs. They could not allow themselves to think about the human costs of their habits, about the children and infants who felt abandoned and unloved by their dope using parent(s), about the brothers and sisters (if they were not also users) who pined for the opportunity to watch TV with them or even to just say, "Goodnight."

No, they could not allow those thoughts or thoughts of their own childhoods lost. There was no room in their lives for such now. They were addicts and they could only allow themselves fleeting excuses as to why they do what they do.

Many had long ago graduated from excuses into acceptance, and a lot of those individuals wore their addictions as a badge of honor symbolizing their complete contempt for the straight world. Time was short before their bodies would force them into sleep, and while awake, they had to concentrate on feeding their habits and not letting anything interfere with that. This meant they must almost always be totally focused on acquiring their drugs. In fact, the only times they ever let such focus slip from their minds was when they were actually doing the drugs.

Doing the drugs was their time of reward for starving their bodies for days, for going sleepless for multiple nights in a row, for enduring the cops, for risking jail or death by selling their asses or doing smash and grabs and for allowing the world to look upon them as vermin. That these things were evil, wrong, bad, unhealthy, or even too heavy of a price to pay never once occurred to most of them.

The girls knew they didn't feel good about selling their asses and the guys knew they didn't like getting caught and spending time in jail, but for the most part that was the extent of their concerns. Life and pain are cheap to an addict. They become even cheaper when compared to the high that the drugs offer them. Cocaine is an anesthetic for their hearts, minds, and bodies, but sadly, not their souls, and like any anesthetic, it only kills the pain for a short time.

Each of these girls has a heart and a soul. It is easier to find in some than in others because each of them has come to drugs in her own way, but while each has a unique story, most of the stories are strikingly similar.

Before drugs became a power in their lives, before drugs could cover their hearts and mask their fears, before drugs became the only tolerable solution of which they could conceive, before drugs worked their way into their systems and became the reason for their existence, long before all of this, some trusted authority figure in their lives violated that natural right given him by God and man, and forever damning his soul, violated these then innocents, either sexually, physically, emotionally, verbally, or all of the above.

It is memories of those violations and the fears of those memories that set in motion a chain reaction that seized their hearts, stole their minds, and offered their bodies to anybody who had forty dollars. It is memories of those violations that stole their self respect, and almost forced them into drugs to find any happiness in their lives.

The often unvoiced cry of the street girl junkie is, "Don't touch my heart; you will hurt it, but anything else is available for the right price." Such is the power of abuse in their lives. Drugs are their anesthetic of choice and prostitution is merely the most expedient way to acquire that anesthetic.

Life and pain are cheap on the street, but relief is not. No, relief has a price and when that relief is drugs, the price they pay is total control of their lives.

The dealers know this and know how to exploit it. Sometimes it is exploited with malice aforethought, sometimes with instinctive ignorance, and sometimes with pure greed, but it is almost always exploited by the dealers and by the abusive boyfriends.

Doc knew how to exploit it perfectly and combined all the reasons. A long time drug user himself, Doc originally got into drugs via steroids and as a way to augment his strength for boxing. He had dreams of representing Canada in the Olympics and going on to a successful professional career thereafter. One day in the ring, though, while thinking about the beatings he had taken from his dad as an eleven year old, instead of covering and countering, he simply covered and kept on covering.

He didn't know it at the moment, but it was the end of his career and of his dreams. He fought for another few months, but not with the heart and the drive that once defined his style. Gone were the quick counter punches, the flawless footwork and the ring smarts.

They had been replaced by the slower movements of an overly muscled competitor who relied more on steroid strength than speed and by the dull mind of a frustrated man whose body no longer responded the way he knew it should. Also gone was his desire to compete; it had been replaced by anger as he now saw his dad's face in every opponent and couldn't figure out whether to pummel him to death or to try and earn his love.

His career on the ropes and his dreams fading, Doc turned increasingly to drugs to ease his pain, and the more he did drugs, the more his career waned. At first, it was crack cocaine. He had seen it at the local Toronto gym in which he trained, so it was not unfamiliar to him.

The first time he smoked it, he used an old soda pop can. By punching four or five pin holes in the side of the can, covering those holes with ashes from a cigarette to act as a filter and melting the rock on top of the ashes, he could fire up the rock, draw smoke through the pouring hole on the top of the can and make it function as a makeshift pipe.

Crack addicts are wonderfully creative in their abilities to manufacture ways of smoking their dope. This is just one of their McGuyveresque methods and is a way that all have tried and many revert to on occasion just to alter the feel of their high. As Doc drew the smoke deep into his lungs, the dope drew Doc even deeper into the black abyss of addiction.

After smoking it at an ever increasing pace for several months, Doc found himself needing more and more money to support his habit. To do so, he turned from petty crimes to dealing. He became a small time dealer in Toronto and also became well known to the local police. It didn't bother him any though; every addict, whether dealing or not, is well known to their local police.

What forced Doc out of Toronto, bringing him west, was that he ran afoul of many of the larger dealers in Toronto from whom he bought. Instead of buying from just two or three of dealers, he was buying from six or seven and running up credit lines with each of them. Owing money to too many dealers for very long is not safe. In fact, it can shorten life expectancy faster than doing the drugs themselves, especially in a major city.

The multiple credit lines and the multiple dealers had been necessitated by the fact that Doc had also begun to do heroin, known on the street as "down" because while coke creates an edgy, jumpy high, heroin brings the users back down, mellows them out a little with a much softer high. Some start using heroin for just this reason, others simply to find a different high than that produced by cocaine.

Heroin, like coke, can be used in many ways. Doc's choice at the time, and the most common method among users in the earlier stages of heroin addiction, was to smoke it. In most cases, smoking it meant putting the powder on a piece of thin tin foil and lighting a flame on the underside of the foil.

This causes the heroin to go up in smoke and the user ingests that smoke by sucking on a straw or a hooter (a home made straw that is held directly above the smoke, often fashioned by just rolling a piece of paper into a round tube). In street parlance, smoking it in this manner is known as "chasing the dragon" because as the flame heats the heroin, the heroin begins to run away from that heat causing the user to have to chase the burning powder around the foil with his hooter in order to always stay directly above the smoke.

What is left over on the foil is a blackish or brownish trail of residue, depending on the purity of the heroin, showing the exact path it took as it ran from the heat. Due to the manner in which heat dissipates from its immediate source outward, this trail is always a non-intersecting, complex curve of some kind that users say reminds them of a dragon's tail.

Doc quickly graduated into rigging though, and soon his arms and legs were full of track marks as veins disintegrated and calluses built up on them from his body trying to protect his blood flow system. Addicts prefer banging (shooting) to smoking because none of the dope is wasted and the rush from a direct injection is more intense.

The other addictive part of shooting is that the addict ends up addicted to what is called, "the feel of the steel." Simply put, it is the excitement of actually playing with the needle and in most cases it becomes addictive to a ritualistic degree because it replicates the experience of preparing the dope, leading to anticipation which is itself somewhat exhilarating.

Anything surrounding the dope becomes an addiction. The simple act of scoring, requiring somewhat clandestine activity, becomes an addiction because of the excitement generated by the risk and by the anticipation. Even doing the crime that generates the money with which to score builds the excitement and anticipation.

Everything about dope is addictive. This is why it is such a difficult addiction to kick. It infects every facet of the addict's life.

Back to Doc though, Doc used and sold both heroin and cocaine. Although both drugs create highs, crack cocaine and heroin create vastly different reactions in the body and are far different in their addictive qualities. Coke is a psychological addiction causing no physical withdrawal symptoms.

Heroin, on the other hand, creates a strong physical addiction, the withdrawal from which is very severe. While crack cocaine is almost instantly addictive psychologically, heroin requires three or four days of use to alter the body chemistry enough to force withdrawal symptoms upon those who do not get their fix.

In street vernacular, suffering psychological withdrawal symptoms from coke is known as "jonesing," and suffering physical withdrawal symptoms from heroin is known as being "down sick" or just "sick." Addicts who are jonesing or who are getting down sick will say or do almost anything to get the drug they need.

This was the life to which Doc was now tied. He was caught between the psychological need for coke and the physical need for heroin.

Doc died alone, lying in the recesses of a cold, dark alley one winter night, wrapped securely in the arms of a heroin overdose. When he was found, he didn't have a penny on him; his coat was missing, as were his shoes and his obituary. Nobody cared.

Normally, a body found in the open air of an alley would gain mention in the newspaper, but it didn't; these types of deaths were all too common and society did not want to be reminded of the cast offs hidden where they would not be seen if nobody looked or acknowledged them.

Nobody cared because there was no time to care; there were drug habits to support. His fellow addicts could not decide whether to mourn him or be happy for him that the misery they each knew all too well was finally over for Doc.

A week later, nobody even spoke about him. He had suffered through the not atypical life and death of a drug addict, a life devoid of joy followed by a sad and unnoticed death.

SECTION TWO

Living with, testifying against, and profiling a psychopathic murderer who will be coming to a street near you soon

Confucius: To know what is right and not do it is the worst cowardice.

Albert Einstein: "The world is a dangerous place to live; not because of the people who are evil, but because of the people who don't do anything about it."

CHAPTER 4

I HELPED PUT PRINCE AWAY FOR THE SAKE OF JUSTICE

William Shakespeare: "….what dreams are left when we have shuffled off this mortal coil…"

Theodore Roosevelt: "In any moment of decision, the best thing you can do is the right thing. The worst thing you can do is nothing."

Mahatma Gandhi: "We win justice quickest by rendering justice to the other party."

Lois McMaster Bujold: "The dead cannot cry out for justice. It is a duty of the living to do so for them."

Why did I testify against Wyatt Prince? I did it because it was the best thing I could do; this was never about some idiotic street code and never about my disdain for Prince, but among other reasons, this was about Paul and about justice. If you are too dull witted to comprehend that, then throw this book away now because you are too much of a drongo to understand even a single word of the truths and humanity within it.

I assisted Prince in putting himself in jail for murder because one cannot take another life without consequences, because Paul was someone's son, someone's grandson, someone's husband, someone's father, and maybe someone's brother or uncle; because those who loved Paul deserved justice (as if jail time for Prince could ever give them that), because Paul's family will never know what might have happened with Paul's life, because they will always wonder what might have been and because they deserved a chance to know and to continue to hope, a chance that Prince's brutal and selfish act forever stole from them.

Now, instead of hopes for triumphs and glories that might have been, Paul's family is left with a horrible memory, the memory of Paul's violent and senseless death at Prince's hands. It is a memory that will haunt them, that will send them searching their souls, trying to figure out if there was something that they might have done to prevent Paul from being there at that moment when Prince decided that Paul's life was less important than Prince's own freedom and Paul's money.

In truth though, such questions would represent false guilt for Paul's family because Paul chose his path in life, just as Prince chose his path, and no person is accountable for how another free person lives his life. Still, even if Paul's family is able avoid or set aside any false guilt, they will now live their lives with nothing but "what ifs" to substitute for Paul. This is what Prince did to them.

As time passes, their "what ifs" may perhaps be fewer, but they will always be there every time they think of Paul. Prince didn't take just one life that night; he also took a family's hopes and dreams and replaced them with nightmares and despair.

So, I did this for Paul's family, whom I do not know. I did it praying that this might hasten the time when their haunting questions may subside a little. I did this thinking about my family and what I would want, and need, for someone to do for them.

I also did this for Paul, whom I did not know either; I did it because Paul deserves some measure of retribution for the future Prince took from him, for the aspirations that Paul will never have the chance to realize.

Everybody has within them some vision of a future, and everybody is entitled to the opportunity to pursue that vision, no matter how unlikely it may seem and no matter how feeble their efforts or their chances to achieve it might appear to others. Prince forever stole that opportunity from Paul, and Prince did so with arrogance, with callousness, with disdain, and with no signs or expressions of remorse.

Prince seems to live his life looking for excuses to feel wronged so he can strike out with violence to cover his lack of efforts in life with a false sense of manhood. When you live as violently and angrily as Prince does, when do you stomp somebody's head one time too often?

I did not seek this responsibility; it was thrust upon me. There was no glory to be taken from this battlefield that Prince created as it could yield no winners, only losers of varying degrees. This is because it was not a field of honor, but rather a field of death, despair, and deceit. It had to be; it was a battlefield born only of drugs.

Thus, the responsibility of this was not a yoke from which I could morally run. It was an onus that was forced upon me when Prince came to my home within minutes of that murder, when he said that he had done it to avoid going to jail for his home invasion because his victim wouldn't stop screaming, when he told me how he stuffed Paul's body in a closet; and when he demonstrated with pride, a day or so later, how he choked Paul, stretching his arms out and making a squeezing motion with his hands; and when he talked about Paul having clawed at his, Prince's, face, and eyes as Paul fought for his life; and how he, Prince, also bit at Paul's fingers and hands, neutralizing Paul's desperate efforts to survive.

Eventually, I think, I hope, that I might look back on what I did here with more pride than grief for my role in helping to find justice for Paul's family, but now, as I write these words, more than anything, I still feel the burden created by my having had to protect my roommate from the street as Prince and his courtroom goons told all that my roommate is a goof and a whore, and continued to terrorize her after the trial for doing that which she had no choice but to do after Prince had put her in a no-win position. I am proud of my roommate for her courage and I always will be.

As you read this, please do not allow yourself to interpret any of what I say herein to be excuses; I make no excuses for what I have done; I need none; neither will I offer any apology, because none are necessary either. Excuses and apologies are sentiments expressed by those who have done something wrong. I have done right here, by every standard, not wrong, and I am only giving reasons.

I have always judged right from wrong based on whether or not I would want my kids to know what I had done. By that standard, and other standards, I have done much that I regret, but frankly, I would be forever ashamed to stand before my children and tell them that I was too lazy, too selfish, too weak, or too scared to take a stand for justice on this matter. That being the case, I shudder to think how I might feel when someday I stand before The Lord on judgment day had I backed away from this dirty duty.

So, I stood up and spent eighteen months before Prince's arrest looking into Nietzsche's abyss, knowing it was looking back at me, and handled my responsibilities, and I am fully prepared to live or die with the consequences of my actions.

Now, it is time for Prince finally to handle his responsibilities and accept the consequences of his actions. A good start on that would be for him to finally man up and realize who really put him in prison. That realization comes with a reality check and a mirror.

You also need to think about this for a moment. Paul was not a gangster, not a violent criminal or a thug of some kind running the streets with other thugs. He was a working stiff who at some point made the mistake of doing a rail or snorting some heroin and ended up addicted, losing his way in life, and having to mentally fight his addiction daily.

There is an important distinction between the Pauls of the world and the gangsters. When gangsters arise in the morning, get dressed, and pull on their kicks, they know that before the day ends that this might be their last day, that something in their chosen lifestyle might get them murdered before the next sunrise and they live their lives with the abandonment that accompanies that realization. It is a risk they freely assume when they choose to be a tough guy who lives with violence daily.

When Paul got up that morning, he didn't think he was doing anything that could get him killed. He wasn't going around strong arming people or worrying about a rival gang coming at him; he was just a normal guy, trying to support his drug habit, and, yes, worrying about his family. Without a doubt, Paul was at risk of an overdose, but the reality is that he probably never really thought about that, drug addicts rarely do.

So, there is an inherent difference between the gangsters of the world getting murdered and the nonviolent addicts of the world suffering that same fate. I believe it is that difference that added to making Paul's murder even more of a tragedy and that cried out even louder for justice for Paul.

CHAPTER 5

I ALSO TESTIFIED AGAINST PRINCE FOR YOU AND FOR THE STREET

Voltaire: "**Every man is guilty of all the good he didn't do.**"

Holocaust Museum, Washington, DC: "**Thou shalt not be a victim. thou shalt not be a perpetrator. Above all, thou shalt not be a bystander.**"

I also did this because each community automatically develops, what for a lack of a better term, are "morally acceptable norms." By way of example, selling drugs appears to be a morally acceptable norm in the community comprised of drug users ("the street"), as among other things, does shoplifting, beating women, burglary and robbery.

These morally acceptable norms are created by a complacency of those who are members of that community to enforce, through peer pressure, a particular moral code; and instead, allow their community to become tolerant of some aberrant behavior or another, thereby allowing that aberrant behavior to continually reoccur under protection of silence imposed by a "street code" that commands, "do not rat."

For me, I see "the street" as its own little community, of which I was a part of due to where I lived and due to some of my associations created by my unwillingness to abandon my roommate to a life without a home. Accordingly, having chosen my environment, I was not willing to sit idly by and allow cold-blooded murder to become a morally acceptable norm there.

I fervently hope that those who learn of my actions in the foul murder of Paul will take the same stance in the future that I did, and I don't care how odious any of you find certain individuals; it is just wrong to allow them to die as a result of a murder. No individual can be permitted to be judge, jury, and executioner.

This is a stand I will always take. The street needs to understand that while it can sometimes administer its own justice, by whatever standard it deems correct, that there are limits to its power as some acts are so heinous that the law of the street must be superseded by the law of the land. I count the unnecessary taking of another human life among such heinous acts, and I do not give a damn what you or the street thinks.

There is a definitive line between what can be allowed to be a morally acceptable norm, the street's situational morality, and any semblance of real justice. For me, among other scourges on society, cold-blooded murder defines that line.

Perhaps the street needs to reflect on exactly what it takes to strangle somebody to death. To kill by gunshot takes a second or two. Stabbing someone to death might take from a few seconds to fifteen seconds, while choking the life out of somebody, according to the books on the subject, takes, at a minimum, about three minutes.

For the sake of argument, let's shorten that time by one third to just two minutes. Even at that shortened time, that means, at a minimum, that a person could have counted aloud to one hundred and twenty while the life was being choked out of Paul.

Are you ready to start counting and see how long, at a minimum, Prince had a chance not to kill Paul? "1, 2, 3, 4, 5, 6, 7, 8, 9,10, 11,12, 13,14, 15, 16, 17, 18, 19, 20, 21, 22, 23, 24, 25, 26, 27, 28, 29, 30, 31, 32, 33, 34, 35, 36, 37, 38, 39, 40, 41, 42, 43, 44, 45, 46, 47, 48, 49, 50, 51, 52, 53, 54, 55, 56, 57, 58, 59, 60, 61, 62, 63, 64, 65, 66, 67, 68, 69, 70, 71, 72, 73, 74, 75, 76, 77, 78, 79, 80, 81, 82, 83, 84, 85, 86, 87, ..."

Even the brain dead thugs among you should get it. Those of who still have issues with what I have done need to ask yourself how in the hell Prince could have strangled Paul to death, even if there was no premeditation to start, without Prince knowing he was killing Paul, and therefore, without forming premeditation during the act. Perhaps those sobering thoughts will make you aware of how dangerous Prince is.

If that doesn't do it for you, think about this for a minute. During those two to three minutes, Prince's compatriots had already fled with the money. Therefore, Prince stayed behind to kill Paul so that Paul could not testify against Prince at a future time and because, according to Prince, Prince was worried that Paul's screams, after having been attacked by Prince and robbed by the other two, might bring police.

Then after killing Paul, Prince stuffed Paul's body in a closet, hoping it might take longer to discover, but did a sloppy job in his haste to get away from the crime scene and to chase the money that had been taken. Did Prince know that he had killed Paul, that Paul was dead? Why would Prince try to stuff Paul's body into a closet if Prince thought Paul was alive?

Back to Prince's worry that he needed to kill Paul to shut him up, the reality is that Prince could not know if the police were on the way, or if on the way, whether Paul would identify Prince, and if identified, whether there would be an arrest, and if arrested whether there would be a charge laid and if a charge was laid, whether or not there would be a conviction. So, with about a ninety-five percent chance that there would be no significant repercussions for the robbery, Prince murder Paul to cover the five percent chance that remained.

The next day Prince, bragging to me in a very calm voice, volunteered that he was all right with what he had done to Paul, saying that Paul should have known that he was going to die when Paul chose to fight Prince.

Are you kidding me? Paul didn't chose to fight Prince; Prince jumped Paul from behind for no reason and starting choking Paul. Prince thinks that when he jumps you from behind and starts strangling the life out of you that you should just go ahead and die and that if you chose to fight you deserve to die.

Prince doesn't just live in an alternate reality; he lives in an alternate unreality filled with excuses to blame everything that he does on others. Listening to Prince, it was Paul's fault that Paul died, not Prince's fault.

One of the sadder parts of this entire affair is that the home invasion of Paul was done because a dope dealer decided that because Paul had money, that Paul must have stolen the money from the dealer who stayed with Paul the night before. The reality was that Paul had money because Paul had cashed his pay cheque.

So Paul died because three guys, high on drugs, forgot that when a person works for a living that he gets a pay cheque and because Prince was too cowardly to deal with about a five percent chance that he might get punished for his home invasion.

By the way, Prince's take on the deal was $0.00. That is because while he was hanging back murdering Paul, his fellow conspirators disappeared with all the cash, and by the time Prince caught up with them later that evening the money was all gone. Money in a drug addict's hands has a shorter half life than the wrapping paper on a kid's Christmas gift on December 25th.

CHAPTER 6

PRINCE THE ANIMAL TORTURER

www.peta.org/issues/companion-animal-issues/companion-animals-factsheets/ animal-abuse-human-abuse-partners-crime/: Acts of cruelty to animals are not mere indications of a minor personality flaw in the abuser; they are symptomatic of a deep mental disturbance. research in psychology and criminology shows that people who commit acts of cruelty to animals don't stop there—many of them move on to their fellow humans. "Murderers very often start out by killing and torturing animals as kids," says Robert K. Ressler, who developed profiles of serial killers for the Federal Bureau of Investigation.

"Studies have shown that violent and aggressive criminals are more likely to have abused animals as children than criminals who are considered non-aggressive. (2) A survey of psychiatric patients who had repeatedly tortured dogs and cats found that all of them had high levels of aggression toward people as well. (3) According to a New South Wales newspaper, a police study in Australia revealed that "100 percent of sexual homicide offenders examined had a history of animal cruelty." (4) To researchers, a fascination with cruelty to animals is a red flag in the backgrounds of serial killers and rapists…."

Prince has another side other than cowardly murderer; he is also an animal torturer who broke into my home while I was out of town and tortured my rabbit.

Gizmo was a highly unusual rabbit in that, rather than being afraid of strangers, he loved them. Whenever guests would come by, Gizmo would run to greet them, pushing his head into their feet to gain their attention and to demand that he be petted.

Every night, when I would turn off my TV, signaling that I was going to bed, I would hear Gizmo thumping across the room while making a guttural sound that can only be described as a rabbit purr. Then, he would jump on my bed, run up on my chest, lie down, and lick my face for two or three minutes. Gizmo would then jump down from the bed and scamper under it to go to sleep. It was as if he was saying, "Goodnight, I love you." Gizmo loved me and I truly loved him.

Sickeningly, I remember one night when Prince was holding Gizmo, three pounds of soft, lovable, furriness, and petting him, but Gizmo, as rabbits will sometimes do, decided he was feeling trapped and started to struggle a little to get away. Instead of releasing Gizmo though, Prince held him firmer, and when Gizmo struggled more, Prince then flicked Gizmo on his ear so hard with his thumb and index finger that Gizmo actually squealed and ran around the room several times in fear and in an attempt to shake off the pain. Then, Gizmo scampered under my bed where he hid for the next twenty-four hours, afraid to come out.

Even two days later, when Prince reached down to pet him, Gizmo ran and hid from Prince. I guess Gizmo did not feel the love, just as I did not feel the respect.

What do Prince's actions with Gizmo say about Prince, "If you don't love me, I'll hurt you"? I do not have the words to express how stunned I was and how absolutely revolted I felt and still feel, and I know the message was not lost on my roommate.

The "ear flick" incident finally awakened me to the depth of Prince's brutality, and caused me to think in a new way about the accidents Gizmo seemed to occasionally have had previously, and suddenly, in retrospect at that point, I realized that Gizmo only seemed to have accidents when Prince was alone with him, so from that point on Prince was not allowed in my apartment alone.

Subsequently, there was the time when I was out of town and returned home early and unexpectedly to find Prince in my apartment, after he had broken in and to also discover Gizmo was hiding rather than running out to greet me. Prince, realizing that I knew there was a problem with Gizmo, made a comment to the effect of, *"I don't know what's wrong with Gizmo, but he's acting strange."*

I crawled back to Gizmo who was hiding in the corner underneath some short tables that held my printers to see him in obvious pain, picked him up and ascertained that he was missing a toenail. I then took Gizmo to the vet and was told that somebody had purposely tortured him by pulling out his toenail.

Gizmo was just a rabbit, and incidentally, a rabbit that Prince professed to love and Prince tortured Gizmo for no reason other than his own sadistic pleasure.

CHAPTER 7

THE NIGHTMARE OF LIVING WITH A MURDERER

Choking someone is a very personal way of killing and is indicative of a comfort level in doing so.

The Art of War, Sun Tzu: **"Keep your friends close and your enemies closer."**

My roommate and I lived in a rural area, about fifteen miles from downtown. We had moved there several years earlier because she had expressed a desire to get clean from her addictions, and I believed a rural setting offered her the best opportunity of accomplishing that goal. Because she loved horses and to help her occupy her time, I rented a house with acreage and bought a horse and accompanying tack (horse gear, like saddle, etc.) so she could distract herself from her addictions by going riding every day.

I had originally met her while she was doing her drugs and couch-surfing, and she and I had been living together for some seven years prior to that rural move. Within a few months of meeting, we had formed a relationship built on mutual needs, hers for shelter, money and drugs, and mine for companionship, and she moved in with me in what we agreed was to be an open relationship.

With this understanding, and with mutual caring, mutual trust and mutual respect, we soon formed a bond which grew into what turned out to be a long-enduring relationship, with me providing shelter, food, and whatever additional money I could afford, and with the understanding that she would have to fend for herself beyond my limited budget and that we were each free to form whatever side relationships we might desire.

This move outside of the city was her third effort at getting clean, and as with her previous efforts, and despite the distance from town, her plans to get clean were soon overcome by her desire to get high, and she began drifting into town more and more often and coming home when she needed rest or when her life would became too stormy or chaotic.

It was during this time period that she had met and become enamored of Prince. After meeting him, instead of staying home every night, she lapsed into her old habit of coming home only three or four nights a week and would sometimes drag Prince along with her because Prince had done nothing toward providing himself either a shelter or bed of his own, instead relying almost totally on her for his addictions, food and whatever else he might need or want.

I vividly recall one sunny, summer afternoon, about 5:00 p.m., I was in the kitchen putting the finishing touches on a chef salad after having fed our horse. My roommate and Prince were in her room, supposedly sleeping after she had come home very early that morning with Prince in tow.

I heard a muffled sound from the other room; it sounded like somebody saying, "*Help.*" I poked my head out of the kitchen toward the living room, cocked my ear in the direction of my roommate's bedroom, and heard it again.

Reaching back into the kitchen, I quickly grabbed a sturdy steak knife and crossed the few feet through the living room, headed for her bedroom. As I secreted the knife behind my back and pushed the already slightly ajar door fully open, there was Prince, eyes one foot from roommate's, with two hands around her throat and her face turning crimson red.

Prince looked up, obviously startled to see me, as I yelled, "*Get your fucking hands off of her now.*"

Prince, keeping her pinned to the bed with one hand forcibly on her neck, raised the other hand toward me as if to fend off any advance I might make, and said, "*I'm not doing anything.*"

I repeated, "*Get your fucking hands off of her. Now!*"

Prince then sprang to his feet atop the bed, doing the Muhammad Ali shuffle, and in an arrogant and threatening voice said, "*Oh, you want to step to me, huh?*"

I pulled my hand from behind my back, exposing my weapon to him, while simultaneously raising it above my right shoulder with the flat of the blade pointing skyward as my eyes zeroed in on the exact ribs through which I intended to slip the blade if he advanced or didn't release her, and said, "*I already have motherfucker.*"

Upon seeing I was not just a helpless old man, but was armed and intent on doing what I had to do to defend my roommate, and at the moment, myself also, a startled Prince said, "*Whoa, a knife,*" as he scampered from the foot of the bed, away from where I stood by the side of the bed, exited the room, grabbed his shoes from near the front door, and headed out of my house. Thankfully, I didn't see him again for several days.

Subsequently, my roommate told me that the entire incident had begun because Prince had thought that she was hiding a point of heroin (one tenth of a gram) from him. It should not be lost on you that Prince also chose choking when he killed Paul a few months later, making the strangulation of Paul, as Yogi Berra might say, "*….déjà vu all over again.*"

Within two weeks or so of that choking incident with my roommate, in order to be in a better position to protect her, I gave our horse away to a lady with a nice stable and a big pasture and moved to the downtown core. I remember crying on the front stoop as Ruby was trailered away to her new home.

There is no love more basic or more unfettered than that which an animal gives to its master; how could I not cry as something that pure and innocent would no longer be a part of my life? I think about Ruby often and will always remember her galloping to me excitedly whenever I would come home.

It was a sacrifice that had to be made though because living where my roommate and Prince were spending most of their time allowed my roommate to come home more often, which she did, even though the cost of ensuring her a safe haven was that I had to endure Prince's almost continuous presence.

Sadly and alarmingly, I had often watched my roommate back off from Prince's rage with terror in her eyes and had seen her recoil in fear at his approach, wondering if she had crossed some undefined line of behavior that only Prince's anger at any given moment might determine and scared she might, again, suffer the same torture as my rabbit did when Gizmo rejected Prince or might get choked again or beaten again.

I was forced to become a human thermometer whose only purpose was to measure Prince's level of anger. I knew Prince's penchant for bloodshed, and I knew of other women he had beaten as though they were men, women who had done nothing to hurt him, but had only said something that angered his fragile sense of what he believed respect for him should look like. I had interceded in countless arguments, scaling them down before the violence with which Prince threatened my roommate, violence which I had stopped many times in the past, could arise again.

Prince obviously draws no distinction between the two sexes and their differing levels of defenselessness, as he draws no distinction between physicality and words, or between a real threat and a man (Paul) lying on the floor choked to helplessness.

Prince's anger and his violent disposition made it a constant balancing act when he was around, with an explosion only a misunderstood word away; and with his extreme arrogance, sensitivity and feelings of inadequacy, misunderstandings were common. I am a man and his tirades were frightening to me. How could my roommate not have been scared to death of him, especially after he almost choked her to death?

Knowing Paul's fate later on, I shudder to think what might have happened had I not had that weapon at my disposal when Prince was choking the life out of my roommate as she was faintly calling for help.

My roommate's understandable reaction to Prince was to shirk in fear and knuckle under to his intimidation; mine was to arm myself and prepare to defend her, my home, and myself. I was often scared of Prince, but I have never been and never will allow myself to be a slave to my fears. I will stand up and I will fight and I will die if I must. If you have nothing for which you are willing to die, then you have nothing worth living for.

Part of the reason that I helped Prince into prison is that I could not be with my roommate twenty-four hours a day, seven days a week, and because my roommate does not possess my psychological skills in defusing tense situations or my physical abilities for self-defense. And with Prince in prison, she finally would be safe from his fists, his feet and his choke holds, because she did not need her body and her ego battered anymore, and because she deserves a chance in life, a chance she would never have had under the vituperative, brutal, disrespectful, and perilous tutelage that Prince continually imposed on her.

While I could give a myriad of examples of the menace Prince presents to any who might have the misfortune of encountering him in one of his frequent foul or arrogant moods, or when he thinks he is dope sick or about to be dope sick, or when he is jonesing for crack, or pills, or any dope whatsoever, I, the person who fed Prince and gave him shelter, was sitting at my computer surfing the net and Prince had a question for me. As Prince often did, he expressed his question in an unclear manner, and I asked for clarification.

Disliking not being understood, Prince sprang to his feet, darted up to the front of my desk, which at that point was the only thing separating us, and launched into a rant about respect and disrespect. Without a single word spoken by me, I watched Prince's rage grow, fueled only by the anger that he had created, as he unrelentingly disgorged his vitriol for a full five minutes, violently kicking my desk and demanding that I not look at him.

At that point, my roommate, not knowing that my hand under my desk held a knife with which to defend myself, pushed her way in between Prince and my desk, telling Prince that I had neither said, nor done anything, but Prince continued his flailing, arms swinging, and jutting out from behind my roommate, making it appear as though my roommate might be Devi, the four-armed Hindu goddess, but with a foul mouth.

Prince then repeatedly thrust his head out sideways from behind my roommate's shoulders, screaming that my roommate could not protect me, that he, Prince, would not disrespect my home by doing anything in it, that he had never disrespected me, and that I was a "fucking dead man" as soon as I left my fucking apartment, and that he would see me on the street and "fucking kill" me.

What my roommate did not realize, although her courage to attempt to protect me was appreciated, is that when behind my desk I was in no danger, as understanding who Prince was, I had intentionally arranged my furniture in such a manner that while it appeared that I was trapped in a corner, the reality was that I had a weapon close at hand, and that I was only trapped in the same sense that the occupants of a castle are trapped by a moat. I was unreachable without Prince exposing himself to me.

Those are just two examples out of the scores of times that Prince forced a knife into my hand to protect my roommate, my home, or myself.

According to Prince's stories, he didn't just terrorize and threaten my roommate and me. He told me in graphic detail, of having been hired to collect from a guy who owed a drug dealer money, and how he, Prince, tied the debtor to a chair and burned and tortured him by melting his leg to the bone with a blowtorch.

Did I believe a word he said? No. Whether the story is true or not misses the point though; the point is that you should ask yourself what it says about the mindset of an individual who would feel compelled to fantasize about such a thing or who would fabricate such a tale and tell it in order to attempt to impress others.

Prince had other stories too, stories of burglaries gone bad, of armed robberies, of being hired to do a hit, of getting searched by the cops one night and how they didn't find a sawed off shot gun that he had strapped around his neck, etc.

If any of Prince's tales sound as though they might have been from movies you may have seen, you are not alone, but again, what do those stories say about Prince's fantasies and what do those fantasies say about who Prince really is?

CHAPTER 8

RESPECT ACCORDING TO PRINCE

Respect was only that which Prince deemed it to be at any given moment, changing with his mood.

Confucius: "Without feelings of respect, what is there to distinguish men from beasts?"

Now, allow me to show you some more of what Prince referred to as "respect" in his harangue in the most previous chapter. I had moved to an apartment in the "hood" and allowed Prince to move in with my roommate and me because I wanted to provide my roommate a port of refuge nearby to where she could come if feeling threatened. Also, by allowing Prince to live with us, she would be spending a higher percentage of her time where I was in a better position to protect her. It was less than ideal, but the best I could do given her lifestyle choice and her relationship with Prince.

I had survived a massive heart attack while living in California and had moved back to Canada because of my lack of health insurance in the United States, a move that I had made to save my life due to the free healthcare available to me in my native Canada. I had, at the time Prince moved in, survived five additional heart attacks here in Canada.

Having fought through those health issues, I was unwilling to risk my life by falling victim to a blood infection brought about by Prince's contaminated rigs. Accordingly, my roommate and I each explained to Prince that because I had suffered through those multiple heart attacks that my ability to recover from any infection was less than that of an individual with a healthier heart. We also explained to Prince that his Hepatitis C created even more risks for me, necessitating that he, Prince, be fastidious in his efforts to leave no used rigs around or any possible blood contamination anywhere in my apartment.

Prince promised that he would never leave his rigs or his blood anywhere, that he would always respect my needs and my home. Here then, in the following pictures, is that respect which Prince promised.

Please note, due to a computer crash, these pictures do not include the photo of a dozen or so used rigs waiting to fall on anybody using the bathroom, rigs that Prince had stuck into the bathroom ceiling as though it was a dartboard for his medical waste.

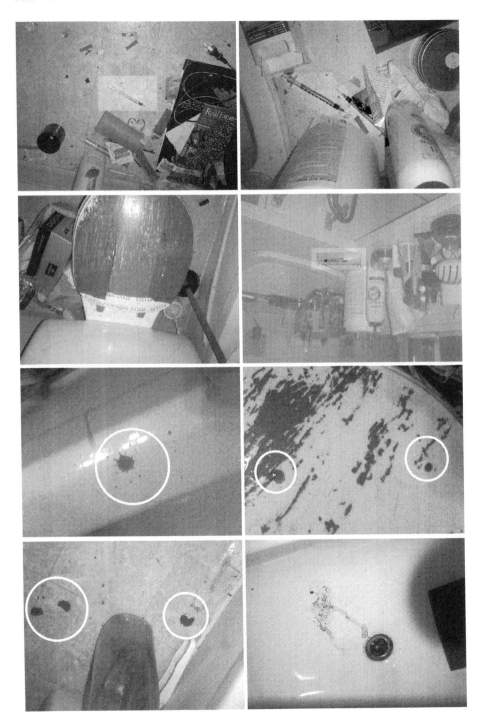

CHAPTER 9

LOVE ACCORDING TO PRINCE

Love might control the giver, but never the recipient or it is not love, but merely a sickness.

Khalil Gibran: "Love passes by us, robed in meekness; but we flee from her in fear, or hide in the darkness; or else pursue her, to do evil in her name."

Now, let us take a terrifying journey into the dark shadows of what love is in Prince's sick mind. Prince used to pretend that he cared about my roommate, telling her that he hated it when she had to go out and earn money. Sometimes, he actually had tears in his eyes as he told her how much he hated it.

If Prince hated it that much he would have gotten up off his slimy, carbuncled ass and taken care of his own dope habit rather than forcing my roommate into the choice of being verbally abused by him because she didn't have heroin for him or being emotionally abused by him because she did what she had to do to get heroin for him. In what was almost a daily occurrence and one that absolutely revolted me, Prince would lay on my floor moaning for twelve or more hours just hoping that my roommate would bring him dope and bitching that she always let him down.

Further belying Prince's declarations of love and any inkling he might have had of the actual meaning of the word, I will never forget Prince sitting at my dining room table one evening, and Prince, in a dreadfully calm voice, detailing how much my roommate was a part of him, and then continuing on, telling me that because of that connection that if he ever knew that he was going to die that he had made the decision that my roommate and he would die together.

At that point in time, he had already decided when Paul should die and was telling me that he would also decide when my roommate would die.

That is love in Prince's world. In Prince's sick mind, people live and breathe only because Prince deems it right to allow it.

Did I believe him? You can bet your first born I did. Hell, I already knew Prince had done one murder and I knew him to be psycho enough that he would not think twice about killing my roommate in some twisted murder suicide ritual.

Anyhow, back to Prince's sick statement. If he had sat there and explained to some stranger on the street who did not know my roommate that he loved his woman so much that he had decided the two of them would die together, that might be one thing. It would still be disgusting, but at least somewhat less disturbing to that person than it was to me.

That wasn't the case though; instead, Prince sat there as if what he was saying was normal, in fact so normal that he thought it wouldn't alarm me in the least, as he told me that he was going to someday kill a woman whom I had promised to provide for and whom I had protected for over a decade.

With Prince, it is all about Prince; he has no sense of anything or anybody other than what he wants and people are just objects that he either finds useful or that get in his way. If they get in his way, he will threaten them, beat them, or even kill them. If they are useful, he will use them until they are broken or until they have given up on Prince's promises meaning anything.

Allow me to show you more love according to Prince's demented mind. I had known my roommate for some twelve years at the time of the occurrence that I am about to relate to you and had watched her steadily and precipitously decline since she had begun her relationship with Prince. So, when Prince sat down one night in June 2009 and told me that because of his love for my roommate that he had worked hard to increase her self esteem, I was dumbstruck.

I wonder what Prince thought had increased her self esteem the most, hitting her, kicking her, choking her, calling her vile names, physically threatening her, or telling her that she was incompetent and stupid?

Thanks to Prince's punches and put downs, my roommate's physical health, her self esteem, and her hygiene were at nadirs that I could never have imagined even two years prior. When my roommate's sister saw her in November 2009, for the first time in two years, her sister wept because of how my roommate looked compared to the last time her sister had seen her, a time long after my roommate had been doing drugs, but before my roommate had hooked up with Prince.

Prince said he loved this woman; I say he loved terrorizing her, stealing from her, blaming her for his own failures, and sending her out to take care of his addictions. I say that he did not love her at all, but what he really loved was controlling her, sponging off her, and intimidating her. Prince is a mentally diseased parasite.

CHAPTER 10

THINGS THAT GO BUMP IN THE NIGHT

Carlos Ruiz Zafón: **"Those places where sadness and misery abound are favored settings for stories of ghosts and apparitions…"**

I have always, at least since my late teenage years, had a faith in God. During some periods in my life, faith may have been less evident to others and less important to me than at other times, but it was still there, if only in the background. It seems to me, that people turn to their faith in times of stress, and living with Prince, a confessed murderer and otherwise violent thug who had often threatened to kill me, could certainly be classified as stressful.

With my faith comes a begrudging belief in the existence of things phantasmal that some might witness in this world, things such as apparitions or ghosts. I do not like to recognize the existence of such because if they are real, I feel somewhat threatened, and I am not certain that I should, by my faith, give credibility to such creatures. I am certain though that I am not to attempt to communicate with said entities.

Thus, I tell you what I am about to describe with a fear that telling you causes you to question my credibility. Nevertheless, it is part of the Prince story, and friends have told me that I should relate this part of the story. Accordingly, with the foregoing disclaimer, you are about to hear of things beyond my comfort zone and beyond my complete understanding. You are about to hear of a ghost.

A few days or so after Prince came to my door following the murder of Paul, my roommate and Prince were sleeping on the floor with their heads pointed in the direction of the kitchen and the adjacent sliding glass door, and I was sound asleep in my bed that was situated on the opposite end of the room near their feet, when suddenly Prince bolted up, and looking my direction, yelled at me, "*What da fuck; why did you fucking kick me in the head?*"

My roommate and I immediately shot upright from our sleep due to the loudness and suddenness of Prince's angry outburst. Prince, while turning to my roommate, continued, "*Hal just fucking kicked me in the head; he came out of the kitchen and fucking booted me.*"

Prince began to stand up, and with his rage at that point, my roommate and I instantly realized that he was doing so in order to exact revenge on me for what he believed I had done to him. As I was wrapping my fingers around the hilt of the large knife hidden under my pillow, my roommate quickly interceded, pointing out to Prince that I was in bed, nowhere near the kitchen, and that I could not have gotten from the kitchen to the bed that quickly without stepping on them because the open space between the kitchen and my bed presented an extremely narrow passageway due to the fact that their bodies blocked what would normally be the path.

After about a minute of talking, my roommate was able to calm Prince; and to my relief, Prince lay back down, finally realizing that I had done nothing. Prince then calmly said, "*It was buddy; buddy followed me home; I knew he did.*"

I asked who buddy was, and Prince responded, "*Paul; he followed me home after I killed him.*" [*Authors Note*: Unlike the U.S. where "buddy" is a name, in Canada "buddy" simply means any un-named male.]

Although the point of this chapter is not to talk about the craziness and risks of living with Prince, it should not be lost on you that one can be laying peacefully asleep, with Prince also sleeping, and moments later might have to be concerned about fending off a violent attack by Prince. Had my roommate not been present at that time to calm Prince, I truly believe there would have been a knifing that night, because I would have had no choice.

Although I had a deep desire to free myself from Prince, to have gotten rid of him in a fatal act of violence was not what I wanted, because for Prince to have died by my hand would have done nothing for Paul's family because they needed to see their loved one's killer face justice in a courtroom.

There were many, many times throughout the eighteen month wait for Prince's arrest that thoughts of Paul's family buoyed my courage enough to force upon me a second or a third effort to calm a situation, rather than to strike back out of a selfish fear for my life.

There were more eerie instances too for which I have no explanation other than a ghostly presence. Being less than young, I could not make it through the night without needing some relief in the bathroom. Because there was no lamp or wall switch proximate my bed, it was my custom to turn off all the lights before I crawled in bed, and to then turn off my television, after having turned the volume to zero, making it the last light source I switched off.

At that point, I would place the remote control on the floor beside the head of my bed so that I could quickly switch the TV back on and use its illumination to safely navigate my way to the bathroom when my inevitable nightly need arose.

A few days following the "kick in the head" incident, I awoke one night and began groping around for the remote control, but could not find it. I pulled myself up and sat on the edge of the bed, waiting for my eyes to adjust to the darkness so I could safely navigate my way to the bathroom without stepping on my roommate's or Prince's feet which extended within inches of the foot of my bed.

As I was preparing to stand, I was startled when the television clicked and then flickered to life. Looking around the room, I then spotted the remote control sitting on the dinner table across the room from me. Either my roommate or Prince had obviously used it while I slept and neglected to place it back by my bed. I ask you, the reader, "Who turned on the TV?"

Over the approximate eighteen month period between Paul's murder and Prince's arrest, there were many other inexplicable episodes, too, as if I was being reminded of Paul's need for me to stay the course in the hunt for justice. My roommate often reported seeing the sheets next to me moving about when I laying still and was sound asleep. Light switches would suddenly turn on or off by themselves, and house guests reported to my roommate or me that they saw a figure in my hallway or in my kitchen. Added to these incidents is that fact that I habitually had the feeling that somebody else was lying in my bed next to me, sensing that presence from a sensation of a sinking of the mattress beside me.

Neither I, nor did anybody else who saw or encountered the ghost in my apartment, with the exception of Prince on the "kick in the head" night, spoke of any sense of trepidation or feeling of malevolence about its presence. Strangely, their reaction was ho-hum, like, "*By the way, did you know there is a ghost standing in the blah, blah, blah?*"

When guests did bring it up, I poo-pooed its existence, and I never spoke of it to individuals who had not encountered it. I could not talk about my growing belief that it might be real and that it was Paul because that would bring up the murder, something that could blow the investigation, and I needed Prince to think that Paul's death had been forgotten and chalked up as being an overdose death.

I can only assume, if Paul's spirit was really in my home, that it departed after Prince's arrest and that it was either because I had done what I had to do or because it wanted to follow Prince to Prince's new housing at the Wilkinson Road jail.

I will never be certain about the mysterious happening in my home surrounding that ghostly presence, and despite the many instances that occurred, I am not certain that I am comfortable saying that there was a ghost in my home. I am sure each of you will make that determination for yourself based on your own convictions; and that, indeed, is how it should be.

Throughout this book you will find simple 'yes" or "no" questions at the end of certain chapters. You are invited to go online and provide your answers to those questions. Your identity will be strictly confidential.

If you want to keep reading instead of answering the questions as they arise, you can always go online after you finish reading and answer all of the "End of Chapter" questions at that time. It is your decision. The questions are present to allow you to express your opinions.

Your answers will be compiled in real time and you can always check back on www.breakingthecode.ca later to see on your opinions compared with those of the other readers. Additionally, your answers might be used in the future to petition the courts and/or government to make certain changes to current laws. This is your chance to have your voice heard and to make a difference.

END OF CHAPTER QUESTION

1. Do you think Paul's ghost was in my apartment?

Post your answer on www.breakingthecode.ca.

CHAPTER 11

OPERATION PRINCE

Jack Nicholson as the Joker: **"Did you ever dance with the devil in the pale moonlight?"**

The seeds for Operation Prince (not the official police operational designation) were planted at about 2:00 A.M. on the morning of April 10, 2009, immediately after Prince had come to my apartment and told me he had murdered Paul during a home invasion with two other guys. It was not until some fifteen months later that those seeds actually flowered into a full fledged undercover operation that culminated with Price's arrest for murder on October 4, 2010. Between those events is a story of stress and anguish.

Allow me to make it absolutely clear right now that up until Prince's arrest, my roommate had zero knowledge of the fact that I had called the police about the murder and zero knowledge that I had been working with the police to see Prince arrested and prosecuted for his crime. Furthermore, there was no way for her to intuit any of the above because she was too busy running the streets with Prince while supporting his drug habit and hers, and I was extremely cautious, leaving no clues of what I was doing.

Additionally, contrary to inaccurate reporting by the Times Colonist, I was paid $35,000, not $40,000, with seventy percent of that due to me when Prince was arrested and the remaining thirty percent to be paid when the appeal period for Prince's trial ended, regardless of the outcome of that trial. In fact, the only ways I would not have been paid is if I was found to have lied or failed to attend any court summoned appearance.

While that might seem like a lot of money to some, in the decades before heart issues forced me back to Canada, I had been a Registered Representative on the New York Stock Exchange, as well as a successful businessman and inventor with five patents under my name, sometimes earning that amount in less than a week. I can assure you that my $35,000 remuneration was never a real incentive and was the most difficult $35,000 I had ever earned, as the eighteen months preceding Prince's arrest were the most trying eighteen months of my life.

At the point in time when the murder occurred, I had known Prince for several years and had always found it difficult to stomach his presence due to his arrogance, his hair trigger temper, and his constant need for attention and dope. But, after the murder, Prince became even more unpredictable, even more insufferable, even more erratic, even more self-centered, and even more violent, as if energized by having killed Paul.

One night, he held my roommate captive at the bottom of the back stairwell in my apartment building while he went through her purse, took her money, told her that if she moved a muscle or said a word that he would smash her face in and then sat there and smoked her dope in front of her before taking off with her cash and telling her she wasn't allowed to leave the stairwell for thirty minutes, or else.

Another time, sitting in my living room with my roommate and me, Prince thought he had crystal bugs crawling in and out of his skin and when neither my roommate nor I could see them, Prince became enraged, screaming at my roommate that she was blind and threatening to kill me because I must know the bugs were there and I was just "*fucking*" with him.

It was during this period of time that I had discovered Prince had been torturing my rabbit, and that I imposed a ban on him being in my apartment unless I was there. This made little difference to him though as he would simply, under threats of violence, refuse to leave when I needed to go somewhere. Instead he would just lay in his bedding on the floor, sniveling and whining until my roommate might come back with some dope for him.

Often times, I would have an appointment to meet my heart doctor or somebody for whom I was designing a brochure or doing a business plan, and Prince would go into my bathroom and narcissisticly comb his hair for thirty minutes, then lock the door and refuse to leave.

If my roommate or I asked him to hurry up, he would threaten to "fucking kill" us if we didn't "fucking" get off his ass. You need to understand that he would be in the bathroom for three hours or more as he took what he termed "a quick shower."

Twice, he actually overfilled the bathtub, purposely clogging the emergency drain thereof with a wash rag or t-shirt and intentionally allowed the tub's overflow to fill the bathroom floor with water, wherein he then bathed himself on the bathroom floor as water continued flowing out into my hallway and into the common hallway of the building, flooding it and flooding the apartment below us. Both times multiple neighbors called the police because as Prince was doing this, he would yell vile rants and improvised raps about fucking all the girls and killing people.

I endured at least two death threats per week by Prince against me, sometimes replete with violent arm waving, with hyper-exaggerated movements and accompanied by his customary invectives, as well as his yelling, door slamming, and furniture kicking. He was an absolute nightmare and cops and management at my door became the routine during this period. I was actually fighting three eviction notices brought about by his behaviors at one point.

With this as a backdrop, my roommate and I had a young lady staying with us for whom we were helping to get a recovery bed and dealing with her parents and her brother, an individual who himself was less than rational at times. I actually spent most of my first payment from the police helping this young lady get into recovery, and although we have lost contact with one another, as of mid 2012 she was clean, married, and had a child of whom I am the godfather.

From my viewpoint, the police investigation appeared never ending because other more high profile cases kept getting in the way and the coroner's office kept getting backed up from other murders in other municipalities.

For a couple of weeks at a time, I would go to eight hours or so worth of police meetings per week, and then suddenly there would be a month or two of deafening and disheartening silence. Even when working with the police as I was, they are an extremely secretive bunch and I was left to speculate on what was happening with the investigation. During all those times, Prince continued bouncing off my walls with his drug use, making threats against my roommate and me, and doing break and enters in the neighborhood, etc.

He never seemed to grasp the concept of not pissing in your own back yard, instead dealing drugs in my apartment building parking lot and the back stairwells, as well as breaking into the underground parking thereof and smoking or shooting up his dope.

The $35,000 was not just an offer I received; it was a result of time consuming and tense negotiations with RCMP professional negotiators who would fly over from Vancouver expressly for meetings with me. After an agreement was reached, there was a contract drawn up that had to be reviewed by RCMP brass, signed by them, and then countersigned by me. The process just surrounding this contract took several months by itself.

Early on the police had offered me a "witness protection" program, instead of a financial pay out. The witness protection program came with stipulations that I accept relocation, a new identity, and a monthly stipend for a period of time.

I was unwilling to travel that road with them because my roommate was still in the throes of her addiction and would have accidentally outed me within a few days due to her activities surrounding her addiction. Additionally, I was not going to allow myself to be put in a position of entrusting my monthly finances to some bureaucrat in a swivel-back chair to whom I was only a statistic, and therefore, possibly find myself indigent in a strange town because of an inadequate stipend. In street vernacular, "That's not the way I roll."

The alternative would have been for me to just up and go, leaving my roommate to fend for herself, and I was not going to reward her years of loyalty with abandonment. Again, "That's not the way I roll". I don't run from my troubles. Accordingly, I made the decision to stand beside her and negotiated the contract spoken of above.

I was questioned about everything surrounding Prince, re-questioned, and then every detail was vetted. I was questioned about my personal life and about my history. The police even went so far back as to find out that I had once written a bad cheque in Topeka, Kansas some forty-five years earlier, a cheque that would have overdrafted my account by less than a dollar. I was also cautioned that any criminal activity by me during the term of my contract with the RCMP could invalidate my contract. The rules were so stringent that I was even directed to update my car insurance when it was noticed that it was due to expire in a few days.

To the credit of the police and to my relief, I was never asked about other crimes of which I might have been aware or about other people I knew. There was a feeling of a single common goal, and at least from the non-negotiators, a level of mutual respect. In my past business life in the United States, I had negotiated multiple hundred thousand dollar deals and was not a fan of the negotiators' tactics.

I was taught how to make proper notes that could be read and would be concise and cogent to the reader, then questioned about those notes during another vetting process after having been put through a scenario the only purpose of which appeared to me to be to evaluate my performance and my honesty.

That note taking skill was supposed to be widely used throughout the investigation because I spent far more time with Prince than was to my liking and needed to memorize any comments made by him and commit them to paper later. Often though, I would simply text the information to one of my handlers, or call him/her directly when the opportunity arose, because actually keeping written notes around was too dangerous with Prince's propensity for rifling through my drawers for money or objects of value that he could purloin and convert to dope or cash on the street.

Because of Prince's violent nature, I was involved in a very serious and perilous project and it was quickly obvious to me that the police were not going to allow any detail to get past them. It was also obvious that the police had a protocol that they were required to follow and that they followed it scrupulously. These were professionals in every sense of the word and left nothing to chance. I am not a stupid man, so I also understood that they needed to be able to cover their asses if something went wrong.

Throughout the entire process, my identity was kept secret from non-team members and I was in their files only by a number, with access to those files being limited to a select few police. In fact, knowledge that I even existed as an informant and that there was an ongoing operation to convict Prince for the death of Paul was limited to very few law enforcement personnel.

Had this been an operation wherein I was not to be required to go public at a later date, I feel assured that my involvement in it would have never been known to anybody other than those individual police with whom I had direct contact or to a handful of their superiors who were directing their actions.

We would meet in motels and never arrive at the motel or leave to motel together. This was a very secure operation, to me seeming overly so.

I was entrusting my very life to those individuals and their respective superiors were entrusting an investment of around a million dollars on my ability to handle my responsibilities and find justice for Paul.

Understanding all of this, then realizing that I was living with a violent and unpredictable madman, and that if I was forced to overtly call the police on him in order to protect my roommate and/or myself, the entire operation might have been unsalvageable because any level of trust Prince might have had in me would have instantly evaporated, I felt the pressure of my responsibility to carry out my assigned duties, as well as to protect my roommate, to protect the young lady whom my roommate and I were helping into recovery, and all the while, having to tolerate the intolerable when it came to Prince's behaviors.

There came a time when the police were in my suite, wiring it for sound and video, and I was not allowed to be within four blocks of my building because I was not permitted to know the identity of the police technicians. Then suddenly I got a call from one of the technicians telling me that some people who thought Prince or my roommate owed them money were trying to kick in my door.

Without consulting the police, I broke the "four block rule" hurried to my building, never entering the suite, and convinced the trio of miscreants who were still in the common hallway that the people they could hear in the suite were higher level criminals who they would be advised not to meet and also convinced them that somebody had called the police on them and that they had better get moving quickly. I then sneaked them into the underground parking and out of a back entrance to my building. (Somebody actually had called the police who were arriving at the front of the building unaware of the covert operation in my suite.)

The discussion (a euphemistic word) that ensued between my handlers and me that evening was not something that either of us probably wishes to elaborate on. (If the police technicians didn't want me to attempt to do anything about those marauders, then why in the hell tell me about them?) I relate this incident to you to give you another dimension to the stress being created in my life by the unpredictability of what can occur when Prince and drugs are part of the equation.

There were a couple of other disagreements, too, and on the rare occasions when they would arise I was at a severe disadvantage because it would be four against one and you know what generally happens to the "one" in that case. These were respectful arguments to be sure, but they were also heartfelt, and therefore, emotionally charged. In the end, though, no matter who prevailed, we went forward as a team with no "I told you so" ever passing anybody's lips.

Despite those disagreements, I knew that the police had my back as much as they could, but with the secrecy considerations I often found myself caught up in a situation wherein any attending cop(s), if I needed to call the police, might misinterpret the circumstances, and perhaps blow the operation in some manner, so I didn't call the police but twice; instead, I just managed things as best I could. There was the additional consideration that the more often the police attended my place on account of Prince, the more suspicious Prince might become.

As weeks were turning into months and months into a year and nothing positive was happening with the investigation, I was becoming anxious and frustrated and wondering if Paul would ever find justice and if my nightmare would ever end.

There even came a time where Prince had to appear before the courts on another matter and I stood Prince's bail for him because Prince going to jail at that point would have brought the investigation to a standstill. I did so because I was not looking for just a short vacation while Prince was temporarily out of my hair, but, instead, wanted this investigation over with and Prince in jail for many years.

I took this action without consulting my police handlers and absolutely of my own accord because I was afraid that I would be told, "No." I was 64 years old, infirmed, and running out of mental, emotional, and physical energy and I needed my life back.

As an aside, while speaking of bail, I remember another time when Prince convinced a friend of his to put up a cash bail for him. The charges in that case were quickly dropped and Prince immediately went to the courthouse cashier, secured the return of the bail money for himself, and called the dope man, thus stealing his friend's money. I do not believe the two ever spoke again. Now, not only do you know the meaning of respect and love in Prince's world, you also know the meaning of loyalty.

Back to the undercover operation though, the investigation had dragged on for such an extended period of time that when it had finally ended there was only one police officer who had started with me who was still part of the operation, Dave Bown, the gentleman with whom I had originally spoken about Paul's murder on the night it had occurred. Dave is truly one of the good guys and I had a lot of faith in him and respect for him because I knew that he had been somewhat instrumental in helping a lady to decide to get off drugs and then to move out of town, away from a slime ball who was abusing her.

Please understand that originally I had thought that I could anonymously let police know that Prince had murdered Paul and then just walk away. This fact is evident in multiple police interviews that were recorded by the police.

I had figured that I had solved the murder and that all police had to do was prove it. I didn't go into this thing looking for a job, for excitement, or for money. I hate working for other people; I had enough excitement in my life, and my finances, as became apparent during the trial, were manageable.

In meetings with Dave and other police officers though, it was made clear to me that the only way that there would be any assurance that Prince would be charged and convicted would be if I were willing to discard my cloak of anonymity and testify.

On one hand, this was not an easy choice because it would be a life changing decision for my roommate and me, a decision about which I could not consult her because of her relationship with Prince. On the other hand, it was a no brainer as Paul needed justice.

I was dealing with a handful of cops, each with their own strong personality, but also with the bond of "brothers under the badge" between them and I needed to believe that there was somebody who could be impartial. So, I agreed that I would come on board, but only if Dave promised that he would walk the entire path with me.

I needed somebody in whom I could absolutely trust before I was willing to put my life on the line, as well as that of my roommate. I was raised that "if you've got a good horse you give it the spurs" and in times of stress we tend to revert to our upbringing for some sense of security, so Dave was my man.

Meaning no disrespect to any of the other officers, but I would not have had anywhere near the same comfort level had it been anybody other that Dave, who had my back, especially because the other officers answered to the large bureaucracy of the RCMP and did not live within the community. Dave was a city cop from a much smaller force and could not just leave town and return to his job in "whereverville," allowing him easily to divorce himself from whatever might have unfolded as a result of the investigation and my participation in it.

I am not a drinking man, but when Prince's arrest finally came, I cracked open a bottle of Johnny Walker Gold that I had been saving for just that occasion, a very well hidden one that Prince had been unable to find when pilfering my apartment, and I drank a solo toast to Paul, to Paul's family, to justice and to an end to one leg of my journey. I slept like a baby that night, but it wasn't simply because of a couple of stiff ones; it was more due to the sheer exhaustion and relief.

The largest burden I had ever felt had just been lifted from my shoulders, but my ordeal was not over yet, and I knew it. There was still a trial to come and the anger of certain brain dead idiots on the street to be dealt with once I testified and my role in the police investigation became known.

CHAPTER 12

THE CASE THAT PRINCE IS A PSYCHOPATHIC KILLER

Identifying a psychopath using the Hare checklist

You have had the opportunity now to begin to understand Wyatt Prince's personality, so I think you may find the psychological profile of him, with my opinions added, very enlightening. See if you agree with me that you have reasons to be concerned about his imminent release.

The Hare Psychopathy Checklist was initially developed to assess the mental condition of people who commit crimes, and it is commonly used to diagnose people who may exhibit the traits and tendencies of a psychopathic personality. Most mental health professionals define a psychopath as a predator who takes advantage of others using charm, deceit, violence and other methods to get what they want.

Robert D. Hare is a researcher in the field of criminal psychology. He developed the Hare Psychopathy Checklist (PCL-Revised), used to assess cases of psychopathy. Hare advises the FBI's Child Abduction and Serial Murder Investigative Resources Center (CASMIRC) and consults for various British and North American prison services.

He is professor emeritus of the University of British Columbia, where his studies center on psychopathology and psychophysiology. He was invested as a Member of the Order of Canada on December 30, 2010.

As you read through the following checklist with my brief descriptions of Prince's behaviors, please recall the details of Prince's actions while he was staying with my roommate and me.

Look for glib and superficial charm –

A psychopath will also put on what professionals refer to as a "mask" of sanity that is likeable and pleasant. For example, the psychopath may do good deeds to gain his or her victims trust. Look for a grandiose self perception. Psychopaths will often believe they are smarter or more powerful than they actually are.

Prince would often hold a door for an elderly lady exiting a store and would do so with a flourish and a giant sweep of his arm as though he was a velvet clad gentleman from the eighteenth century. When one first met Prince, he might create an image of being a "stand up" guy, laying on the charm like a kid pours sugar over cereal, seemingly ready to help you in any way he could.

Watch for a constant need for stimulation –

Stillness, quiet, and reflection are not things embraced by psychopaths. They need constant entertainment and activity. Determine if there is pathological lying. A psychopath will tell all sorts of lies: little white lies as well as huge stories intended to mislead.

Prince was a continuous beehive of activity, almost never sitting still unless sleep deprivation or going on the nod from a heroin fix forced him to inactivity. He was full of stories about running from the cops, about burglaries, about beating people, and about robberies. He would also often claim his role in any situation was greater than it actually had been, adding details if his audience appeared to believe him and becoming enraged if he sensed any skepticism. It was as though he was saying, "act as though you believe my lies or suffer the consequences of your disrespect.

Evaluate the level of manipulation –

All psychopaths are identified as cunning and able to get people to do things they might not normally do. They can use guilt, force, and other methods to manipulate.

Prince is a highly intelligent and savvy (street smart) individual, blending cunning with intimidation and even ruthlessness to achieve his objective(s). Prince would often attempt to lay guilt trips on his friends about how he took better care of them than they took of him and about how he was a better friend than they. When he was down sick, he would moan out loud how sick he was, whining like a small child with a big belly ache. Whether sick or not, he also constantly threatened people and beat people, finding any reason in the actions of others for him to use as an excuse for his own anger.

Look for any feelings of guilt –

An absence of any guilt or remorse is a sign of psychopathy. Consider the affect or emotional response a person has. Psychopaths demonstrate shallow emotional reactions to deaths, injuries, trauma or other events that would otherwise cause a deeper response.

When my roommate's parents passed away, within a few weeks of one another, Prince did not allow that event to alter his need for my roommate to provide drugs for him. After he murdered Paul, I never saw any sign, or heard any expression, of remorse, not even a quiet reflective moment about what he had done; instead, he bragged.

Look for a lack of empathy –

Psychopaths are callous and have no way of relating to those who can actually feel empathy.

It seemed to me that Prince had no way of relating to anybody on any emotional level whatsoever.

Take a look at the person's lifestyle –

Psychopaths are often parasitic, meaning they live off other people.

Prince sponged off of me by latching onto the coattails of my roommate, but more than that he constantly wanted twenty dollars to get unsick and obviously felt comfortable eating my food, living in my home, and never offering a penny, and hardly, a "thank you." He also sucked my roommate dry for all her dope and money, as well as running up debts to dealers all over town.

Observe the person's behavior –

The Hare Checklist includes three behavior indicators; poor behavior control, sexual promiscuity and early behavior problems.

Somebody with a violent, hair-trigger temper obviously has poor behavior control. Prince was with many different women over the years in which I knew him, although he was supposedly true to my roommate. I cannot speak to his childhood record because that is sealed by the courts.

Talk about goals –

Psychopaths have unrealistic goals for the long term. Either there are no goals at all, or they are unattainable and based on the exaggerated sense of one's own accomplishments and abilities.

Prince would talk about getting clean and getting a high paying job in the logging industry, or even becoming a high-end narco trafficker, but he never got off his ass to attempt to accomplish any of those things.

Look at whether the person is impulsive or irresponsible –

Both those characteristics are evidence of psychopathy.

Consider whether the person can accept responsibility. A psychopath will never admit to being wrong or owning up to mistakes and errors in judgment.

After Prince murdered Paul, it was Paul's fault according to Prince; if Paul hadn't resisted Prince, Prince wouldn't have had to kill Paul. Everything negative that ever occurred in Price's life was somebody else's fault. It was his childhood; it was my roommate; it was anybody other than Prince that was responsible for Prince's failures.

Examine marital relationships –

If there have been many short-term marriages, the chances the person is a psychopath increase.

I cannot speak to this as I do not know.

Look for a history of juvenile delinquency –

Many psychopaths exhibit delinquent behaviors in their youth.

Prince had told me stories of crimes he had done when a young teenager, but his youth record is sealed and I have no way of verifying anything in that regard. Additionally, my roommate told me how Prince had told her that as a child Prince had tortured animals.

Check for criminal versatility –
Psychopaths are able to get away with a lot, and while they might sometimes get caught, the ability to be flexible when committing crimes is an indicator.

Prince told me of cons he had run on people, of being a violent debt collector, of armed robberies he had done, even of arson jobs, as well as many break and enters; and Prince's extensive record, at least in BC, but not including Alberta, consists of multiple charges for a variety of crimes.

Check out if a person makes constant use of "the poor fellow's imagery" –
Psychopaths are experts at manipulating our emotions and insecurities into causing us to view them as "poor injusticed fellows," thus lowering our sentimental guard and rendering us vulnerable for future exploitation. If this psychologic resource is continually combined with unacceptable and evil actions, this equals a powerful alert sign about this person's real nature.

According to Prince, he would never have started down his path had his father not been a criminal and had he not been unloved as a child. Prince's life was rife with violence and threats and betrayals of him that an unfair world forced upon him. It was my roommate's fault when he was down sick; it was Paul's fault that Prince had to murder him; it was a bad rig that caused the dope to get wasted; no matter what, it was always somebody else's fault and never his fault.

Pay extreme attention to the person's treatment towards others –
Psychopaths are generally prone to belittle, humiliate, mistreat, mock, and even attack physically (or kill, in extreme cases) people who normally would bring no benefits to him/her in any way, such as subordinates, physically frail, or lower-ranking people, children, elderly people, and even animals - especially the latter ones.

Prince beat on mentally handicapped individuals, on physically handicapped individuals, and on women. He rolled drunks and tortured my rabbit on multiple occasions.

The justice system needs to wake up before it allows another psychopath to wander the streets with little or no supervision. The parole boards need to begin making inmates earn their parole, rather than those boards simply looking for an excuse to release them. I realize that it costs less money to release these twisted individuals early than to keep them incarcerated, but what about the costs of their future victims?

According to leading authorities, even scarier is the fact that evidence shows that psychopaths do not respond well to treatment. In fact, treatment often makes them more dangerous because the psychopath uses the knowledge gained from treatment, such as catch phrases and a deeper understanding of psychology, to become even more expert at manipulation and control.

END OF CHAPTER QUESTION

2. Do you think Prince is a psychopathic killer?

Post your answer on www.breakingthecode.ca.

CHAPTER 13

RUMOURS ABOUT PRINCE FROM PRISON

Never put your trust in the words or seemingly appropriate actions of somebody capable of deluding himself because that person will eventually make a fool of you.

Voltaire: "There are some that only employ words for the purpose of disguising their thoughts."

I cannot comment with absolute assuredness on the sincerity of what is supposedly happening with Prince in prison, or on his allegedly new found faith in God; I can only remind you that Prince is a master manipulator.

Consider the example of when Prince's brother had to come from out of town to deal with a criminal matter before the courts. Prince's brother had done nothing wrong but he had suddenly found himself under arrest in his home town because Prince had given the cops his brother's information when Prince was being questioned one evening.

Please realize the lack of conscience one must have to put your brother's neck in the proverbial noose, and, also, think about how convincing a liar one must be to be able to persuade the cops, absent any identification, that you are somebody else, and finally, recognize the ego it would take to believe that you could sell your masquerade to law enforcement.

Accordingly, I am not a believer in Prince's supposed change of attitude as I see several red flags about its genuineness, indicating it is nothing more than a charade to impress a future parole board. Let's start with Prince's forgiveness of me.

What exactly is it for which Prince forgives me?
1.   Does he forgive me for him torturing my rabbit?
2.   Does he forgive me for his many threats on my life?
3.   Does he forgive me for him breaking into my apartment while I was out of town?
4.   Does he forgive me for him dealing drugs in my back stairwells, creating eviction notices against me?
5.   Does he forgive me for him choking and beating my roommate?

Prince forgiving me seems self-delusional on his behalf and in keeping with his proven proclivity for blaming everything in his life on others. Forgiving me is akin to Prince forgiving Gizmo, my rabbit, for Prince having terrorized and tortured him.

In fact, Prince's statements of forgiveness of me indicate that he has yet to even begin to grasp the reality of what he did, and therefore, bring into question the sincerity of his efforts at rehabilitation and whether his claims of newly found religious convictions can be trusted.

With all this religion and forgiveness floating around, I can't help but wonder if Prince also forgives Paul?

In that religious vein, I recall one evening when Prince was invited to join my roommate and me in our regular evening prayers. It was very early on in the routine of my roommate praying with me and my roommate, not wanting Prince to feel excluded, had asked Prince if he would like to join in.

I will never forget the chill I felt when Prince gloatingly declined, telling my roommate and me that he, Prince, was going straight to hell when he died and that he was fine with that.

It should be noted that in that proclamation by Prince, he did not disavow a belief in God. Thus, his statement was not about a lack of belief in God, or Heaven, or hell, but about a personal assessment of his life and his intentions not to alter his actions in the future.

The reader may believe whatever he/she would like to concerning Prince's supposed rehabilitation; but you, the reader, never lived with Prince. I did. Prince is a very unpredictable and frightening individual, capable of going from a smile to a state of rage within a few seconds.

I know, and have known, many ruthless individuals, but Prince is the first person I have met whom I consider to be truly evil. When Prince's release from prison finally comes, I fear for the public and for anybody with whom he might have contact.

The facts are simple: although some of you might like to think of Prince as a friend, he is really nothing more than a cold-blooded, sociopathic murderer. One can only wonder if Prince will come out of prison with a teardrop tattooed under his eye or whether he is too vain to accept a tattoo on his face.

That doesn't make any difference though because every time I think of Prince, I will see the blue stained outline of a teardrop tattooed on his cheek along with the excitement forever frozen on his face at the moment that he bragged to me about having murdered Paul.

Let me ask all you street code preaching haters a couple of questions. When was the last time you thought of Prince? Did you like him?

Were you afraid of him? Do you know anybody other than a couple of drama queen sluts who might miss him? I miss the cyst that the doctor cut from my ass, but I don't want it back. Do you want Prince back?

END OF CHAPTER QUESTIONS

3. Do you think Prince has found God?
4. Do you think Prince is a changed individual?

Post your answers on www.breakingthecode.ca.

CHAPTER 14

A MESSAGE TO PRINCE

You represent everything that I find repugnant and evil in a human being

Of late, there are rumors from prison that you have turned your life around, that you no longer do drugs, that you are actively participating in prison rehabilitation programs, that you have found The Lord, and finally, that you forgive me for what I did to you.

I do not need your forgiveness. If there exists any sincerity in your words of forgiveness and if you have really found The Lord, you need to ask The Lord who really needs forgiveness instead of lying to yourself about the need to forgive me.

Wake up, man up, and take responsibility for your own actions; it was not I who put you in jail, and it sure as hell was not Paul, who, contrary to your statements, did not choose to die simply by choosing not to shut da fuck up or by choosing not to "go gently into that good night." It was not your parents; it was not the courts or the police; it was not drugs; it was not your childhood; it was not my roommate; and it was not your buddies who ran from the crime scene that night.

It was you, and only you. You are the one who allowed yourself the excuses to kill. So fuck you and your alleged forgiveness of me. I have done nothing to you that might require your forgiveness. Take your forgiveness, dump it into one of your dirty rigs, and shoot it up your infected ass.

You are where you are because of the choice you made that night to put your freedom ahead of Paul's life. Unlike Paul, though, your life continues and you will have the luxury of more choices to make.

So, when you lay your head on your pillow at night, remember that there is an individual who will never need a pillow again due to your lack of boundaries and due to your cowardice to face the consequences of your home invasion. And remember, not just in my world, but in any world, even on "the street," there is right and there is wrong, and what you did was wrong in the minds of all but the brain dead, by any and all standards.

Don't bother to dive headlong into a cesspool of self pity or make up a thousand excuses either. I do not feel sorry for you, and I know of nobody who really does.

Instead, accept the consequences of your actions; and whenever you begin to lament where you are, remember Paul, and remember Paul's last gasps for life; remember Paul, and look to heaven and beg God's forgiveness. It is God who must forgive you, but absent your sincere repentance, He will not.

You can choose to hate me, or you can choose to hate your actions. I will tell you that in both the short term and the long term, you will be far better off choosing to hate your actions. If you chose the path of hating me, it will not bother me one iota, for I need neither your respect nor your friendship, and I look forward to the day when my memories of you will be tucked away in the darkest recesses of the deepest closet of my mind.

However, if instead of hating me, you choose to hate your actions, perhaps you may reach deep within yourself and find the strength and the courage to realize that you deserve to be where you are, and that out of the two people whose paths crossed that fateful night, you are the lucky one because you still have what you forever stole from Paul: you have life and hope.

After reading all of what I have to say, if you still want to reach out from your cell and call me names like "goof" and "rat," then do so loudly and do so clearly. Scream your lungs out; for those of us who care about our fellow humans, though, your screams will go unheard, drowned out by Paul's whispers for justice.

They are whispers that echo in our hearts and our heads, and they will always be louder than your threats, your excuses, and your cries for mercy. You showed no mercy and you deserve none.

I did what I did out of necessity, and therefore I did it without guilt, without shame, and without remorse; and today, these many years later, I still feel the same way because I did what I did with reason and with cause, and I did it knowing that God was watching.

END OF CHAPTER QUESTION

5. Do you think Prince should be granted early release or probation?

Post your answer on www.breakingthecode.ca.

SECTION THREE

Understanding the justice system, those who haunt its halls in the name of news and those who look to it for an excuse to commit mayhem under a supposed street code

Louis D. Brandeis: "If we desire respect for the law, we must first make the law respectable."

When authority is coupled with ignorance, arrogance, and intolerance, justice is always the first victim and innocents are always in greater danger than they need be.

Fiat justitia, ruat caelum. *(Let justice be done though the heavens fall.)*

Francis Bacon: "If we do not maintain justice, justice will not maintain us."

CHAPTER 15

THE COURTS NEED TO UNDERSTAND HOW VARIOUS DRUGS AFFECT INDIVIDUALS

Author's Note: This chapter is included in this section in order to give the reader a greater understanding of the effects that various drugs have on the mind because that understanding is necessary for the reader to comprehend the material in the chapters that follow.

There is no such thing as a life-long, weekend warrior. Anybody using hard drugs for any period of time will end up in the depths of a destructive addiction.

Gordon Lightfoot: "…sometimes I think it's a sin when, I feel like I'm winnin' when I'm losin' again…"

If you have simply heard about drugs and do not understand how various drugs affect the behaviors of the users thereof, it is time to clear up the many misconceptions of those who have seen too many movies or too much television. Let me make it perfectly clear that I am not talking about the medical effects of drugs in this section, but about the behavioral effects.

There are three basic classes of street drugs, excluding marijuana. Each of the three categories induces its own behavioral patterns in the majority of users. The three main categories are what are termed as "up," "down" and "sideways."

Up is cocaine in powdered form or cooked into crack; down is any opiate or opioid (a synthetic opiate produced for pharmaceutical purposes), principally heroin followed by morphine, followed by various pills. Sideways is crystal meth, a highly addictive and dangerous combination of lye, ammonia, iodine, phosphorous, ether, ephedrine and drain cleaner.

Before delving into the behaviors attached with each, allow me to put to rest one myth. You have all probably seen individuals on the street/ sidewalk, swaying back and forth and standing around almost falling down, but recovering their balance, only to do the same thing every few seconds. Their motions almost seem ape like as they contort their face or bob their head.

Many of you might believe that you are witnessing a drunk or a reaction to drugs. You are probably not. You are likely witnessing the effects of sleep deprivation as the body tries to fall asleep and the individual's mind attempts to fight the body's demand for sleep.

This sleep deprivation is brought on by many days without sleep, sometimes as much as a week or more with only a few hours of sleep. People in this condition might be uncomfortable to look at, but are not a threat to you as they cannot even stand up right, let alone chase you, rob you, or harm you.

Because in most cases the only way visually to determine if somebody is actually high on drugs, as opposed to sleep deprived or drunk, is to observe the dilation of that individual's pupils. The odds are that if you sat down next to somebody who was simply high on drugs and not sleep deprived, and had a conversation with such a person, you would not even know that person was high. Think of, among many others, actor Heath Ledger, Phillip Seymour Hoffman, or Cory Monteith. Their drug overdose deaths came as a shock to the public because the public did not know they were addicts.

Because these individuals were all heroin addicts, and because if you are addicted to heroin, you must have heroin every four to six hours, three hundred and sixty-five days a year, it becomes obvious that at some point all these actors performed for the camera while they were high.

So, if you think that you can tell if someone is high, ask yourself two questions: Number one, understanding how heroin demands daily use by the addict, do you really believe now that none of those actors appeared in shows or movies you saw and that they were not high on drugs in any of those scenes? Number two, how can truly loving and concerned parents not know that their child is using drugs?

The answer is obvious; people high on drugs can effectively hide their addictions, can function quite normally, can have lucid conversations, and can even think about their actions and the possible results of those actions. In short, they can plan, form intent, and act on that intent.

If they could not, then they could never rob a taxi driver, a store, or even an individual or ever shoplift or ever commit rape or murder. It is the psychological freedoms that drugs create within them that are the reasons some Hollywood actors become addicted.

Thus, it follows that nobody committing any of these illegal acts could have been even close to the near catatonic state of the stumbling individuals discussed above, and therefore, has the ability to form intent.

While it is true is that somebody high on drugs might be emboldened by those drugs or might have their natural inhibitions suppressed to some degree or another, this does not relieve that individual from any responsibility for the consequences of his/her actions that he/she thought through.

So what are the behavioral effects of the various drugs?

Heroin - The short-term effects of heroin abuse appear soon after a single dose and disappear in a few hours. After an injection of heroin, the user reports feeling a surge of euphoria ("rush") accompanied by a warm flushing of the skin, dry mouth, and heavy extremities. Following this initial rush, the user goes "on the nod," an alternately wakeful and drowsy state. Mental functioning becomes clouded due to the depression of the central nervous system. Other effects are slowed and slurred speech, slow gait, constricted pupils, droopy eyelids, impaired night vision, vomiting, and constipation.

(From: www.drugfreeamerica.org)

Cocaine - Crack causes a short-lived, intense high that is immediately

followed by the opposite—intense depression, edginess, and a craving for more of the drug. People who use it often don't eat or sleep properly. They can experience greatly increased heart rate, muscle spasms, and convulsions. The drug can make people feel paranoid, angry, hostile, and anxious—even when they aren't high. Regardless of how much of the drug is used or how frequently, crack cocaine increases the risk that the user will experience a heart attack, stroke, seizure, or respiratory (breathing) failure, any of which can result in sudden death.
(From: www.drugfreeamerica.org)

Crystal Meth - The drug's effects are similar to those of cocaine but longer lasting and more intense. Crystal Meth can cause erratic, violent behavior among its users. Effects include suppressed appetite, interference with sleeping behavior, mood swings and unpredictability, tremors and convulsions, increased blood pressure, and irregular heart rate. Users may also experience homicidal or suicidal thoughts, prolonged anxiety, paranoia, and insomnia.
(From: www.drugfreeamerica.org)

CHAPTER 16

THE COURTROOM LAWYERS IN THE PRINCE MURDER TRIAL

Kimberly Henders-Miller – Crown Counsel

Mike Munro – Defense Counsel

Kimberly Henders-Miller

According to the internet, "During her career, Kimberly Henders-Miller has prosecuted a wide range of cases, ranging from traffic tickets to murders. In addition, Kimberly sits as the Chair of the Crown DNA Resource Group for the province of British Columbia and is an Executive Member of the Canadian Bar Association's Victoria Criminal Justice Section. She enjoys mentoring junior counsel and supervises articled students during their time in the crown counsel office."

I found Ms. Henders-Miller to be professional, on top of the facts, dedicated to her job, caring, and as ethical of an individual as I have encountered since returning to Canada some fifteen years ago. I was especially struck by an ever-present feeling that Ms. Henders-Miller had a lot extra hidden behind her eyes, things she would only use if needed.

I made a decent living for some three years playing cards and I am glad that I never had to play poker against this most impressive lady.

Beyond that, I am extremely grateful to Ms. Henders-Miller and her very able assistant, Leslie Baskerville, for the sincere respect they always showed my roommate, a respect not often enough given to those with addiction problems.

Mike Munro – Defense Counsel

Mike Munro is a fixture around the courthouse, often acting as a Legal Aid attorney, and therefore, well known to the many addicts who avail themselves of his services. Although Mr. Munro can often be found conducting an actual trial, he has gained a reputation for being a plea bargainer for his clients.

CHAPTER 17

MADAM JUSTICE SUSAN GRIFFIN'S TWO MOST REVEALING STATEMENTS

Author's Note: This chapter and the next are about my opinions concerning one judge's comments at one specific trial, and as such are not intended to make generalizations about her or about her character. They are simply meant to analyze her comments, and thereby, in the only manner available to me, to correct the public record which she created. While I still have a sincere respect for the courts, I no longer have any respect for this judge.

In the next two chapters you will see justice gone awry as a judge gives an individual just convicted in her courtroom of homicide more respect than the citizen who risked his life to bring that criminal to justice. I believe illogic by the judge resulted in a sentence that was too lenient for his crimes.

Chief Justice Warren Burger: **"Ours is a sick profession. [a profession marked by] incompetence, lack of training, misconduct, and bad manners. Ineptness, bungling, malpractice, and bad ethics can be observed in court houses all over this country every day."**

Plato: **"Knowledge without justice ought to be called cunning rather than wisdom."**

Marcus Tullius Cicero: **"I prefer tongue-tied knowledge to ignorant loquacity."**

To start with, please understand that when rendering a verdict and speaking about the proceeding that led to that verdict, a judge is instructed by law, "*When the factual implications of the jury's verdict are ambiguous, the sentencing judge should not attempt to follow the logical processes of the jury….*"

Thus, if there is <u>any ambiguity</u> as to what a jury might have thought to reach its verdict, a judge, in passing a sentence, is limited because of that ambiguity as to what he or she is allowed to attempt to understand concerning the jury's thinking. That limitation was in place regarding my testimony in Prince's trial unless the jury's verdict was NOT in any manner ambiguous, but instead, pointed unequivocally to the jury believing or disbelieving my testimony.

With that in mind, subsequent to the jury having found Prince guilty of manslaughter, instead of the greater charge of murder, if Madam Justice wanted to question my honesty, she was required, by law, to build a platform from which to do so and their would have been no plank available to Madam Justice with which to build that platform unless the jury's verdict was consistent "*only*" with it having rejected my testimony.

Accordingly, Madam Justice stated, "*The jury's return of a verdict of not guilty of murder but guilty of manslaughter is consistent with the jury rejecting Mr. Hannon's evidence as to what precisely Mr. Prince said to him after the death of Mr. [name withheld for privacy]. If rejection of his evidence is <u>only</u> consistent with a verdict of not guilty of murder, then I too must not accept Mr. Hannon's evidence.*"

The problem is that Madam Justice was dead wrong in her above stated analysis, and if she didn't know that, she should have. After all, the actual sentencing came approximately two months subsequent to Prince's conviction, meaning that Madam Justice had that entire period to contemplate Prince's sentence, to contemplate the reasons for that sentence, and to contemplate exactly what she would say in her <u>Oral Reasons for Sentence</u>.

Madam Justice's erroneously self-serving thinking becomes clear when you study the following logic: I testified that Prince had told me that he, Prince, had strangled Paul to shut him the fuck up, or words to that effect. I did NOT testify as to whether or not Prince shutting Paul up meant just rendering Paul unconscious or actually killing Paul.

I did testify to the fact that Prince had told me that Paul should have known he was going to die when he chose to resist Prince, but while that is highly suggestive of an intention by Prince to kill, it is not a definitive statement as to Prince's intention at the moment he was strangling Paul.

Therein lays possible reasonable doubt as to what Prince's intention was when strangling Paul, and that slight difference was a question that the jury needed to answer for itself as it was an aspect of the decision of the jury to which I did NOT and could not testify.

Accordingly, the jury could have concluded from my testimony that Prince may have strangled Paul with the intention of rendering Paul unconscious, thus shutting him up as far as Paul's screaming at that moment went, or that Prince strangled Paul to shut him up permanently. It was the jury's decision to make and either decision by the jury would have been consistent with it having believed my testimony.

So, the jury could have believed every word I spoke and still found that Prince did not intend to murder Paul, thus finding him guilty of manslaughter instead of murder. Accordingly, Madam Justice was NOT required to reject my evidence, and in fact, was not even allowed to attempt to follow the jury's reasoning in reaching its verdict because the jury's verdict was NOT consistent "*only*" with a rejection of my evidence, but could have been consistent with it accepting my testimony and merely interpreting Prince's words to mean one thing rather than another. In other words, since the jury could have found as it did while believing my testimony, Madam Justice did not have the right to attempt to follow its thinking or to reject my evidence.

Madam Justice simply used false logic concerning what the jury's verdict meant in regard to my testimony to grant herself a permission that did not exist for her, the permission to reject my testimony by stating that the jury did not believe me and that therefore, she was also forbidden to believe me. Using that false permission, she then called into question my integrity and my motives and began a series of insults about my credibility, insults which you will soon see, do not even come close to passing any test of logic.

Looking again at Madam Justice's statement by which she granted herself permission to reject my testimony, please note that the phraseology she uses clearly refers to everything I said "*after the death of Mr.....*", thus encompassing almost my entire relevant testimony as I was in court to talk about what Prince had said to me after the murder, not prior to it.

So, first Madam Justice gave herself permission to vilify me by ignoring the word "*only*", then she painted the broadest possible guidelines as to exactly what part of my testimony she had permission to call lies. Having sat on the bench for many years, Madam Justice is a very savvy and cunning woman.

In this chapter, and next chapter, I will show you how Madam Justice used her self-granted permission to attack me and I will dissect Madam Justice's consistently ludicrous and disrespectful attack on me by comparing it with simple logic. I will also dissect some of her other ridiculous statements.

While the foregoing discussion might have been somewhat difficult to follow, please allow me to start the rest of my analysis of Madam Justice's statements with a comment by Madam Justice that I believe should be less complicated and should serve as an "aha" moment to all by revealing what I believe to be a festering anger and bias against me by Madam Justice due to my roommate's relationship with me (more on that later), and therefore, what I believe to be the very reason why Madam Justice built her false platform in the first place. In an overt attempt to skewer my credibility in front of the courtroom, Madam Justice stated, *"He [Mr. Hannon] seemed unusually motivated to try to have the police focus their investigation on Mr. Prince..."*

Before parsing that statement and others to follow, as you read my arguments regarding this judge's many comments, please take notice of the fact that by the very title of Madam Justice's oration, Oral Reasons for Sentence, she was identifying any comments she made in her oration as reasons why she chose the sentence upon which she decided.

Returning now to Madam Justice's statement that I was *"unusually focused"*, this statement by Madam Justice is undeniably the most monumentally inane argument against my credibility that anyone might imagine.

Indeed, I was highly motivated to have the police focus on Prince. I don't know if I would have used the word, *"unusually"* as did Madam Justice. After all, had you had Prince confess to you on multiple occasions, as he did to me, I'm pretty sure that any of you would have acted as I acted and told the police exactly that which Prince had told you.

Since Prince had stated to me that he was alone during that murder because his compatriots had left the apartment prior to it, I had no reason to even consider the idea of suggesting to the police that they look at anybody else as a suspect. In fact, under the law, it would have been Obstruction of Justice had I suggested to police that they look at somebody who I knew did not commit the murder or who I did not believe might have committed the murder.

When relating to the police exactly what Prince had told me, I also told the police about the two other individuals that Prince had said committed the robbery with him, but who had left before the murder, even naming those individuals. From that moment forward, although I don't know it with certainty, I feel quite comfortable in stating that the police, of their own volition, probably focused their attentions on Prince as the primary suspect. Why wouldn't they?

While I might be just an ole country boy in my heart, and while I may have come into town on a truck, it wasn't recently, I didn't fall off of that truck, and it wasn't a turnip truck, so I'm pretty sure that what Madam Justice was stating was that my testimony would have been more credible to her had I violated the law by lying to the police, thereby sending them on a wild goose chase.

The last time I heard such claptrap from an intelligent individual, George Bush was standing on an aircraft carrier in front of a sign that read, "Mission Accomplished." Later editions of that photo op picture were computer altered to remove the sign. I am delighted that Madam Justice can't use a similar process to cover her blunders, for they are a well documented part of a public record.

If there is any comment by Madam Justice that clearly demonstrates a prejudice against me, it must certainly be that comment that my focus on Prince showed I lacked credibility. Frankly, had it not been for the organized structure of Madam Justice's arguments against me (further detailed below), she might have seemed more of a blithering blatherskite than a cunning judge intent on assassinating my character.

With the kind of bias, or if not bias, certainly illogic, demonstrated by Madam Justice with that objection to me, I pray that she does not represent the future of justice in Canada because even should you decide to discredit any other argument(s) that I make herein, you cannot ignore the world class idiocy of Madam Justice's statement that questions my credibility because I did not mislead the police.

I have a hard time believing that a sitting judge could make such a cretinous statement, but once you factor into your thinking that Madam Justice is an educated individual and then conduct even a cursory analysis of that statement by her, you must, as do I, rightfully question her motivation in raising such a specious objection to my testimony, and therefore, you must also scrutinize everything else Madam Justice had to say about my testimony, and interpret her opinions only after filtering them through the light of what that statement reveals about Madam Justice's mindset regarding me.

Further, when did she make this statement? Wait for it; here it comes; she made this statement A-F-T-E-R every witness who was examined as to exactly who had murdered Paul verified that I was correct about Prince having committed the murder and <u>after</u> the jury had found Prince had committed the murder. So, Madam Justice was stating that I had no credibility even though I was correct about what had occurred and about who had committed the crime. In my world, people gain credibility when their words are proven true, but in Madam Justice's world, my being correct appears to have been a justification for Madam Justice to criticize me.

As you read on, please do not lose sight of the fact that Madam Justice's comments are almost invariably presented in a manner that leaves her squirm room, i.e. *"There was evidence that <u>could have</u>...", "...<u>seemed</u> exaggerated...", "He* [Hal Hannon] *<u>seemed</u> unusually...",* and *"He* [Hal Hannon] *<u>may also have</u> said things..."* She does a deft job of saying nothing definitive, thus preparing herself to have a counterargument to any criticism of her statements. Where I grew up, we called it being "wishy-washy" and we gave little credibility to those who were too afraid and ineffectual to speak their mind, or put in simpler terms, who couldn't simply say exactly what they meant.

Please realize the potential repercussions to the justice system with those types of weak statements and with such obviously flawed reasoning because this judge sits on other cases. Frankly, the damage she can do is scary to contemplate.

With the above as a backdrop and a window into Madam Justice's predisposition, I will now turn my attention to some of her other torturously ridiculous comments which either fail to properly reflect the testimony given in her courtroom and/or fail to pass any test of commonsense.

CHAPTER 18

MADAM JUSTICE'S CONTINUED NON-SENSICAL OPINIONS

Without facts on their side, the biased often resort to character assassination through innuendo.

Clarence Darrow: "Justice has nothing to do with what goes on in a courtroom; justice is what comes out of a courtroom."

Voltaire: "Prejudice is opinion without judgment."

Mark Twain: "Get your facts first and then you can distort them as you like."

Albert Einstein: "Whoever undertakes to set himself up as a judge of truth and knowledge is shipwrecked by the laughter of the gods."

Now let us examine the following comment by Madam Justice, wherein she bloviated by framing her statement to make no definitive point as she continued to call me a liar,   *"Mr. Hannon's evidence during trial seemed at times exaggerated..."*

Let's examine that statement.   Something can only be judged an exaggeration when compared to something else. For example, for testimony in court to be deemed *"exaggerated"*, it must be compared to somebody else's testimony about the detail(s) being testified to or compared to actual physical evidence or compared to what the individual classifying it as *"exaggerated"* knows to be the truth.

In the case of my testimony, I was the only person present when Prince told me what he told me; therefore, I was the only person to testify about my conversations with him. Accordingly, since there was no other testimony with which to compare my testimony about those conversations, Madam Justice could not have judged my testimony about those conversations to be *"exaggerated"* based on any other testimony.

Consequently, it is necessary to analyze my testimony regarding Prince's conversations with me as my testimony related to the physical evidence at the actual crime scene. My testimony in this regard matched perfectly in every detail. Since you, the readers, were not in court, the proof of this is that had it not matched, Madam Justice, a woman obviously intent on disparaging me, would have pointed to any discrepancy with absoluteness, rather than with a hedging word such as *"seemed"*, and she would have pointed specifically to it as being inaccurate or as being a lie, as opposed to simply referring to it as *"exaggerated."*

With those facts in mind, the only remaining item to which to compare my testimony was the "truth"; therefore, Madam Justice must have been stating that my testimony *"seemed exaggerated"* when compared to the truth. The problem with Madam Justice's statement then becomes that she had no truth with which to compare my testimony unless it was only her own truth.

When testifying in court whereat you are sworn to tell nothing but the truth, is exaggerating not like being a little pregnant? You are pregnant or you are not, and you are either telling the truth or you are lying. In other words, Madam Justice saying that I was exaggerating was nothing more than a less than clever way to falsely call me a liar, because she could have had zero knowledge of any "truth" with which to compare my testimony and because the only evidence not created by her in her own mind supported my testimony.

I think that people should expect something more from Madam Justice than that she imagine something and then use that imaginary conception as evidence to which to compare my testimony, thereby creating her own evidence for the sole purpose of taking me to the proverbial woodshed.

Madam Justice also said, "*There was evidence that could have raised a reasonable doubt as to Mr. Prince having the necessary intent for murder, namely: evidence as to the possibility that he was impaired by his drug use…*"

Really? Madam Justice needs to educate herself on the effects of drugs on the mind as she obviously thinks that somebody high on drugs cannot form intent, if indeed, Prince was actually high at the time, something that nobody has established. An addict with a $200 a day heroin habit, which Prince was, does not get high by doing a mere $20 heroin fix anymore than you get drunk from a single beer.

Let us take a minute and further dissect this "*doubt*" due to impairment about which Madam Justice spoke. By her words, Madam Justice believes that Prince could make a plan with two other guys, execute on that plan to the point of starting to choke Paul, but not be able, at any point during that choking, to form the intent to kill Paul.

Does not being told of a plan, participating in that plan, and then executing one's assigned role in that plan show the ability to form intent? In fact, is it not absolute proof of the ability to form intent? I point this out because Madam Justice also said, "*I therefore find that the robbery plan was initiated by Mr. [name withheld for privacy], but was known to Mr. Prince who joined the plan. This was the purpose behind Mr. Prince's choking of Mr. [name withheld for privacy] upon the three men entering the apartment.*"

Madam Justice's reasoning, as revealed by her comment, gets even sillier though because according to her, in spite of his alleged drug use immediately prior to the robbery and murder, Prince had the mental capacity to form the intent to participate in a robbery, wherein Prince's role was to choke the victim during the home invasion and to follow through with that plan, but because of his alleged drug use, some scant ten minutes later and roughly two minutes into the event while choking Paul, Prince may not have the mental capacity to form the intent to kill him.

An analysis of that statement by Madam Justice seems to indicate that she believes she is able to determine the exact moment at which somebody loses the ability to form intent. That is an absolutely ridiculous position for even an uneducated individual to espouse, let alone somebody who must have graduated from college and law school.

Being high on drugs means that decisions could be made to do things that one might not otherwise do; it does not mean that the person is a brainless idiot incapable of thought, decisions, or intent.

Now, back specifically to Prince and how supposed drug impairment might have affected him, perhaps Madam Justice should have gone to the internet, maybe looking at a site akin to www.drugfreeamerica.org to have begun to understand the effects of the various drugs on a person's thinking before she determined something as important as a manslaughter sentence based on her ignorance of the effects of drugs.

Madam Justice obviously does not understand what being <u>high</u> actually means, perhaps thinking of it as being akin to some sort of extreme drunkenness from alcohol or even the presence of a zombie effect in users. Being high invokes a feeling of superiority, sometimes anger, and sometimes paranoia. Further, specifically in the case of heroin which is classified as a "downer" and often referred to on the street as "down", it tends to mellow one out and make one easier going immediately after its use, not to make one uncontrollably violent.

After listening to her, I can only wonder how Madam Justice thinks the scores of rock stars high on drugs could ever form the intent to perform a song on stage and actually execute on that intent. I also wonder if Madam Justice ever watched a Corey Haim, Heath Ledger, River Phoenix, Robert Downey Jr., Phillip Seymour Hoffman, Judy Garland, or Bela Lugosi movie, or any other movie with one of the hundred or more heroin addicts who performed on screen while high, and remembered there lines to boot, as well as were able to emote.

Additionally, if using hard drugs is antithetical to forming intent, one can only wonder if the light bulb or the phonograph was an accident because Thomas Edison was an opium (the base active ingredient of heroin) addict, if modern psychiatry was a misbegotten fantasy because Sigmund Freud was an opium addict, if Madam Justice would have bifocals with which to read because Benjamin Franklin was an opium addict, or if Madam Justice could have thought of counting the ways she is loved because Elizabeth Barrett Browning was an opium addict. Of course none of this speaks to other opium addicts such as Arthur Conan Doyle, Charles Dickens, Florence Nightengale, or a host of other luminaries, but I think I have made my point.

Returning specifically to Prince again, further proving my point of how one can be possessed of a very functional mental capacity while high, if indeed Prince was high, a fact, which again, nobody had established, the evidence showed that immediately subsequent to the murder, Prince had the presence of mind, and therefore had the intent, to attempt to hide Paul's body by stuffing it in a closet, as well as the acumen to avoid the elevator cameras, and instead, to use the stairways to return to the apartment from which the raid on Paul had been launched.

Prince also had the mental wherewithal to be worried about having left behind his DNA, as well as the intellect to "go to ground" until the heat had settled down and to do so away from the building in which he had committed his murder, namely in my building and in my apartment.

Accordingly, Prince was thinking quite lucidly and Madam Justice's assumption that Prince may have had a diminished mental capacity, as were many of her opinions and assumptions, was ludicrous. By the evidence, Prince's mind was functioning perfectly, perhaps even at an elevated level of awareness, buoyed by the adrenalin from his kill.

Therefore, without even considering any other aggravating factors, had Madam Justice had the first clue about the effects of drugs, she might have come to a different conclusion regarding sentencing, something she may well have done had she not seemed focused on destroying my name.

In my opinion, some of what took place in Madam Justice's courtroom subsequent to the conviction of Prince would have been laughable had it not been so lamentable. Madam Justice's unnecessary opinions, unsupported by the facts, were an affront to me because she openly implied that I had lied on the stand.

The jury was the trier of facts, not Madam Justice, and the individuals of that jury were the ones to assess my credibility, not Madam Justice, because her inveighing against me was antithetical to her instructions as a judge and served no purpose whatsoever; the jury had already decided the case and my credibility should have had no bearing on her sentencing.

Also for the record, I did not come to court seeking Madam Justice's approval; I did not require her validation before court; I did not require it during court and I do not require it now; I respect the face I shave every morning.

I came to Madam Justice's court, having put my life at risk for the previous thirty-four months (the elapsed time between Prince having committed the murder and the date of Madam Justice's issuance of her learned opinion, and this does not take into account future threats and attacks which were assured to come, and which did come.)

I came to Madam Justice's courtroom with the truth as my ally and seeking only justice, and while I am profoundly disappointed and angry about Madam Justice's obviously attacking remarks, I, nevertheless, find a measure of self accomplishment in what I did.

Now, let us dive further into Madam Justice's statements. Despite Madam Justice's characterization of my relationship as, "....*he had previously been in a long term relationship with Mr. Prince's girlfriend."*

I have a news flash for Madam Justice, there was no testimony that my roommate's relationship with me had ended, thus, Madam Justice's statement characterizing my relationship with my roommate as "*previously*" was incorrect according to testimony at the trial. I was not allowed to be present during my roommate's testimony in court, and therefore, I make this statement based on my roommate's post trial statements to me concerning her testimony.

Before continuing with the subject of Madam Justice's inaccuracy in using the word "*previously*", I would like to add this thought as to a possible reason why Madam Justice seemed so focused on and offended by my roommate's relationship with me.

Madam Justice's history seems to indicate that she may have a problem tolerating certain relationships. For example, she sentenced an abuser who had severely beaten his wife to a twelve year sentence and Prince to only ten years. Although I agree with the long sentence for the wife beater, I am just comparing the severity of the crimes and the disparity between sentences.

How can a beating, no matter how severe, be considered worse than a home invasion and a death? One is left to wonder what sentence Madam Justice might have meted out had the woman died. Among other examples of Madam Justice's disdain for what she considers inappropriate attitudes in a marriage or simply inappropriate attitudes about relationships, also please see

http://metronews.ca/news/vancouver/630271/korean-billionaires-sexist-attitude-toward-women-factor-in-vancouver-divorce-case/.

Madam Justice needs to understand that the nature of relationships has changed while her hair has been graying for the past three or four decades. Nobody is forced to wear a scarlet "A," and men and women actually cohabitate without marriage.

Back to Madam Justice's lapse of memory now, keeping Madam Justice's inaccuracy in mind and realizing that Madam Justice also made it a point to question my credibility based on a small number of my statements at the actual trial that did not, "verbatim", match my precise testimony given earlier at the preliminary trial, I would like to remind Madam Justice that at the trial I was being asked to recall conversations and events from some two and one half years previous, conversations that were at the trial even older than they had been at the preliminary trial, I was not being asked to recall precisely what I had said at the preliminary trial.

There is an important distinction between the two, and Madam Justice, of all people, should have understood that fact. Madam Justice should also have known that one's memory regarding the precise words used in a conversation can vary slightly over time, but what is important is the meaning of what was said, and whether an individual said, "might" or "may" is really irrelevant.

Furthermore, for me to have attempted to recall my previous testimony from the preliminary trial, instead of answering questions based on my recollections, at that moment, regarding the events about which I was being questioned would have been dishonest, and therefore, perjurious.

Additionally, as most experts agree, when statements concerning complex matters match too closely it is evidence of rehearsal-driven memorization, especially when testifying to conversations some thirty months previous, or even older. Accordingly, everything I said in Madam Justice's courtroom was consistent with me being a forthright individual.

Throughout my interviews with police, my interviews with Crown, and both trials, my testimony remained consistent, that Prince had told me the he had choked Paul to shut him up, whether Prince said to shut him "the fuck up," to shut him "the hell up," or just to shut him up does not matter and does not impact credibility.

There are even police notes to verify the time at which Prince told me that he had choked Paul to shut Paul up, because as was testified to, I repeatedly called police and had them take notes so I would not have to attempt to remember hundreds of comments and conversations over an eighteen-month period, and because, with Prince living with me, it would have been even more dangerous than my then current undertaking for me to have taken notes and kept those notes in my home. Perhaps Madam Justice didn't think that I was taking enough risks with my life already by living with Prince and reporting to the police about him.

I just have this to add about Madam Justice's insult to me based on her logic of my failure to have "total recall," if one is deemed dishonest because he/she could not precisely recall every detail of long ago conversations and events, what does that say about a judge's credibility when that judge could not remember the status of my relationship with my roommate from a hearing at which that judge had just presided over only a few months earlier, especially when that judge had access to the transcripts of both the preliminary trial and the actual trial before rendering any decision or commenting on the reasoning for that decision?

Let us now examine Madam Justice's next objection to me, namely, my offering to allow police to electronically monitor my apartment. Of course, I offered to do so, and in fact, did not just offer it, but encouraged the police to set up surreptitious video and audiotape recordings in my suite.

I needed to protect my roommate, to see to justice for Paul's murder, and to get a violent killer, Prince, out of my life and off the street as soon as possible; and therefore, was more than willing, even solicitous, of having the police record in my suite hoping that the police doing so might lessen my load by hastening Prince's arrest.

I was living with a drug addicted, conscienceless killer who was growing more violent, more paranoid, and more unpredictable every day and who had threatened, on many occasions, especially since his murder of Paul, to kill me, and to "fucking murder" me.

Needing Prince out of my life, a videotaped confession by Prince of exactly what he did seemed the most efficient way to achieve that goal. Trading places with Madam Justice, assuming that she had the guts to do what I did, which I sincerely doubt, would she have wanted to continue to live with Prince for even one second longer than absolutely necessary or would she have offered the police the opportunity to gather as much evidence as possible as quickly as possible?

Let's think this through a little further though. If, as Madam Justice implies, I was exaggerating or fabricating evidence, why would I offer to give the police proof of my alleged chicanery by subjecting myself to video and audio recordings of those alleged transgressions?

As was so often the case in her ex cathedra speech, Madam Justice's premise was entirely devoid of logic. Had I had been lying or otherwise misleading the police, I would have attempted to hide such transgressions, rather than offer to allow the police to have them memorialized on video tape.

Continuing on with another of Madam Justice's comments about me that she offered in her public courtroom as a fact that influenced my credibility, "*Mr. Hannon was paid by the police for his role.*"

Damn…. according to Madam Justice, not only was I a liar, but I was a paid liar.

While Madam Justice obviously did not recognize that living with Prince and having to maintain his trust was a severe detriment to my income, which even though I sometimes bought used electronics from drug addicts and applied my computer skills to other ventures, was to a substantial degree derived from doing business plans, brochures, and promotional work for various companies and individuals, I think that you can appreciate that having a business client stop by my apartment while Prince was raging about getting shorted on his last heroin deal or was in the bathroom doing a fix would not have been the best thing for my business image, and therefore, Prince's presence was costing me significant income, as well as potential future earning. Accordingly, due to the fact that I could not leave Prince alone in my apartment or bring clients to my apartment, I had to put much of my business on hold.

Additionally, as stated, I lived with a drug addicted, violent, self-confessed murderer for some eighteen months after he had confessed his murder to me, risking my physical safety and my life every day. Would Madam Justice not want to get paid for that had she done the same or would she think it part of her civic duty to risk her life, daily?

I don't see Madam Justice refusing her pay cheques because of civic duty. Does the fact that she gets paid for her role in the justice system lessen her credibility?

With this comment by Madam Justice about me being paid, it is almost an unavoidable conclusion that Madam Justice was attempting to leave the impression that I was being paid for the efficacy of my testimony as that efficacy might have related to a conviction. That was not the case and Madam Justice knew it when she continued her, too clever by twice, tactic of trying to destroy my credibility and my reputation with her false premises.

Madam Justice knew that one of the stipulations of my contract with police, of which she had a copy, was that my pay would be forfeit if I was dishonest or lied, and another was that, barring any dishonesty by me, my pay was guaranteed whether or not Prince was convicted. Thus, money could not have been an incentive for me to lie. Contracts with the police always have stipulations of that nature, but generally it is the defense that uses the *"paid by police"* ploy as a reason to question a witness's credibility, not the judge.

Furthermore, let me ask you who you think would be the more honest witness, the guy who would lose a chunk of money if he lied and might also face perjury charges, or the guy who would lose no money if he lied, but might face perjury charges?

Finally on this point of me getting paid, is Madam Justice suggesting that the police suborned perjury, trying to get me to say something I knew not to be true? If so, where is the perjury charge?

If Madam Justice claims that she is not saying or implying that, then what earthly difference did it make that I was paid by the police if there was no subornation of perjury and if lying would have invalidated my contract, and therefore, why bring up that point in her summation of her Oral Reasons for Sentence unless to further falsely attack my credibility? And since it was brought up in the context of her oral reasons, I can only wonder, as with her other criticisms of me, what in the hell it had to do with her sentencing decision?

Now, let us dig even deeper into Madam Justice's analysis of my testimony. Because I was one of the earliest, within hours of it occurring, to alert the police that the death of Paul was a robbery gone bad resulting in a murder, and because I knew that Paul's body had been moved to a closet, and because I knew the cause of death, knew the names of the three people involved in the robbery, knew two of them had left the scene with the money before the murder, as well as other details, it is obvious that Prince told me these things, especially because Prince was the only person present during the actual murder, and more especially, because the facts at the scene both collaborated my statements to police and my testimony.

Accordingly, with the knowledge demonstrated by me, above, a knowledge demonstrated within minutes of the murder, we know Prince must have talked to me in detail about the murder. Therefore, is it not strikingly obvious that Prince could very easily and very understandably have told me why he strangled Paul? In fact, Prince seemed eager and excited to tell me about what he had done as if he wanted to brag to somebody.

The facts are that my evidence concerning the manner of Paul's death, the circumstances with Paul's body, the fact that there had been a successful robbery and the fact that the other two robbers had fled the scene prior to Prince killing Paul had to have come from one of two places, either from

Prince, or from the police, but wait…. the police could not have told me about Prince and about any other participants or the identity of the other two intruders because all the police knew at the time when Paul's body was discovered is what was at the crime scene itself, and they could not even know it was actually a crime scene until I told them because no autopsy had been performed as of then.

Then what are we to make of Madam Justice's opinion when she stated, *"He [referring to my testimony] may also have said things that were informed by information learned after the fact."* What was Madam Justice talking about with this objection/accusation?

She cannot have been talking about when Prince made his statement of intent to me, because as I testified to in court, Prince made that statement a day or two after the murder. Therefore, since everybody knew that my testimony about Prince's statement of intent was made sometime later, Madam would NOT have used the word *"may"* had she been talking about that. Ergo, she must have been talking about the statement which Prince made to me about the murder scene and the other participants.

The problem with this accusation by Madam Justice is that I just proved a few paragraphs back that my knowledge regarding the actual events on the night of the murder had to have come immediately following the murder. So, Madam Justice has stuck her foot in her mouth yet again.

As if she had not yet made enough false allegations against me, Madam Justice continued marching forward, but this time not with pointed insults to me, but with a general description of my testimony as being *"fraught with difficulty"*. Madam Justice knew exactly what she was saying with that snide comment and with all her other scurrilous remarks about my testimony. I think from the analysis so far that it is abundantly clear that what was *"fraught with difficulty"* was Madam Justice's logic, not my testimony.

Now, let's take a closer look at the video surveillance in my apartment. While it is true, as Madam Justice points out, that Prince made no inculpatory remarks, Madam Justice seems to have ignored a significant part of the video tape, the part wherein Prince's actions spoke as loud as any words might have.

Early on in that video that was recorded by police of Prince in my apartment, I showed Prince a press release about the murder, a press release that had been put together by police specifically for that moment, and which, for the first time, publicly defined Paul's death as a murder.

Immediately upon reading it, Prince sat in stunned silence for maybe thirty seconds, then grabbed a pen and a piece of paper from my desk, and began furiously writing.

Next, having finished writing, Prince handed the paper to me; I read it, and it did include inculpatory content, nothing specifically to do with his intent, but inculpatory nonetheless. In an attempt to preserve the evidence, I crumpled the paper into a ball and tossed it toward the trash bag hanging in the kitchen (missing it), hoping to retrieve it later.

So concerned was Prince about the contents of that paper that he immediately arose from the bed, crossed to the kitchen, snatched up the crumpled paper from the kitchen floor and tore it into little pieces. He then disappeared into the bathroom and the sound of a flushing toilet could be heard.

If I was the liar that Madam Justice would like people to believe, why does she think that Prince retrieved the paper and then ensured that nobody else would ever read it?

Let us examine more of Madam Justice's statements. Madam Justice said to Prince, "*Mr. Prince, you did express remorse. You turned to face the family members of Mr. [name withheld for privacy] in the courtroom and said how sorry you were. I believe that you were sincere in your remorse.*"

Yet again, really? Is Madam Justice joking? Please consider:

1. Throughout the preliminary trial and the actual trial, Prince had never uttered even a single word to The Court other than "Not Guilty."

2. The only other words spoken by Prince were those contained in his obligatory apology to the family, words possibly written and rehearsed with Prince's attorney, and they were words uttered with Prince's back to Madam Justice wherein she could not even see Prince's eyes. From her vantage point, Madam Justice could not know exactly where Prince was looking or what his eyes revealed, if anything, about the sincerity of his words. For all Madam Justice knew Prince could have been looking at the wall behind the family and not the family.

3. The jury had just found that Prince had committed a home invasion robbery and manslaughter; therefore, despite that fact, at that point, Madam Justice, based on nothing other than the sound of Prince's voice, was judging a convicted robber and murderer to be sincere.

4. Further, Madam Justice could see Prince's extensive criminal record to which Madam Justice herself had stated, "*Mr. Prince's criminal record and history does not allow for placing much weight on the sentencing objective of rehabilitation.*" This comment makes no sense in view of Madam Justice's statement that she judged Prince's expression of remorse to be sincere. Is not rehabilitation a natural byproduct of remorse?

5. Moreover, considering Madam Justice's apparent lack of knowledge of how individuals who are high on drugs behave, considering the fact that Madam Justice could not see Prince's eyes, with the eyes being one of the few ways that a trained individual can determine whether or not a person might be high, and also considering the fact that trial had been delayed once already because Prince overdosed in jail (yes, illegal drugs are available in jail), then for all Madam Justice knew, by the evidence before her, Prince was high on drugs when he professed his alleged remorse for killing Paul.

With that backdrop, Madam Justice, seemingly by divine inspiration, determined that Prince was "*sincere*" and that my testimony, uncontested by any witnesses and supported by all evidence at the crime scene, was "*fraught with difficulty.*" It is ludicrous.

I challenge Madam Justice to charge me with perjury if her insults to me were anything other than prejudiced remarks against me because she allowed her moral compass to be so offended by the fact that I had a relationship with a woman approximately half my age that Madam Justice lost her sense of judgment and justice.

In fact though, for whatever reason, even if due to some tilt in her moral compass, if Madam Justice really believed I lied, was it not her duty to have had me charged with perjury or to have had the Wyatt Prince trial declared a mistrial? She did neither. Accordingly, and not at all surprisingly to me, Madam Justice's vitriolic statements about my testimony did not mirror her actions.

I now say to Madam Justice, "Somebody had to correct the record; <u>consider it corrected</u>."

In summation of Madam Justice's twaddle in her <u>Oral Reasons for Sentence</u>, I further say, "If clear and direct talk was a furnace, she would have to move to the Caribbean every winter, and if logic was a pair of galoshes, she would be running around with wet feet every time it rained."

Finally, Madam Justice's Obiter Dictum damaged the very protections of the justice system to witnesses because Madam Justice used the cloak of immunity granted her by her position to repeatedly bully me and insult me, a witness who was only in her courtroom because the police had told me early on that no prosecution of Prince was likely unless I was willing to testify.

Who does Madam Justice expect will ever willingly come forth in the future to do their civic duty and risk their well being if they are to be subjugated to the verbal abuse and disrespect of an ungrateful judge? (That was a rhetorical question only.)

Madam Justice can always find a legal loophole with which to bring suit against me. If she does, and wins, it will be a pyrrhic victory because I am a broke old pensioner, and because I will win the ensuing internet PR battle and will then promote my book from the distant corners of the internet, gaining distribution by billing it as "the book the courts don't want you to read." If Madam Justice thinks I am wrong in my opinions or analyses herein, I challenge her to set up a public, face to face debate with me instead, a challenge I think will not be accepted.

END OF CHAPTER QUESTIONS

6. Would you want to be a witness in Madam Justice's courtroom?
7. Do you trust Madam Justice's opinions?
8. Do you think that I proved my points about the idiocy of Madam Justice's comments/statements which I dissected?
9. Do you think I am justified in feeling offended by Madam Justice's comments/statements about my testimony?
10. Do you think Madam Justice would have come at me in the manner in which she did if she had thought of me as a less marginalized individual or believed that I was literate enough to be able to fashion a response to her insults?
11. Do you think Madam Justice disliked me?
12. Do you think Madam Justice's sentence was influenced by a dislike of me?
13. Do you think Madam Justice gave Prince too light of a sentence?

Post your answers on www.breakingthecode.ca.

CHAPTER 19

DID PRINCE CAUSE THE DEATH OF PAUL?

You be the judge

Please consider the following regarding the title question of this chapter. We know that Prince and two other individuals planned on robbing Paul, that they went to Paul's apartment to do so, and that immediately upon arriving there Prince jumped on Paul and strangled him in his own apartment.

We also know that after the other two individuals left with Paul's money that Prince deposited, or attempted to deposit, Paul's body in the closet subsequent to Prince having strangled Paul.

The question then becomes, "Would Prince attempt to put Paul's body in the closet if Prince believed that Paul was alive?" The answer to this seems an obvious, "No." Why take the time to hide evidence when hiding it could accomplish nothing?

If Paul had still been alive, the evidence of a crime having been committed which Prince was attempting to hide would not have stayed hidden for any reasonable period of time, rendering any attempt to delay the discovery of Paul's body pointless. Accordingly, we know that Paul was dead at the time Prince tried to put Paul's body in the closet.

Furthermore, by Prince's own words, Prince was choking Paul to shut him up. The veracity of my testimony regarding Prince's expressed intentions to me that Prince was trying to silence Paul is born out by the following logic.

If it was not Prince's intention to silence Paul, then why would Prince have begun choking Paul again after the money had already been taken? Instead, why would Prince, in order to follow his two compatriots, not have simply kicked himself free when Paul grasped at Prince's legs and then left the apartment without initiating the second choking incident?

Now consider this, if Paul was not dead, then Prince would have only temporarily silenced Paul, as opposed to having silenced him forever. Thus, I draw the conclusion that when Prince began choking Paul the second time, after the money was already gone, it was Prince's intention to kill Paul. [*Author's Note:* I believe Prince meant shut Paul up "permanently" because I know Prince, but the jury, not knowing Prince as I did and not being allowed to be told of what I knew about him, could have understandably decided it was only Prince's intention to shut Paul up temporarily by rendering Paul unconscious and I cannot fault the jury if that was the reason that it came to the conclusion to which it did.]

I think that what happened is that Prince became instantly enraged as I have seen him do countless times before, and that Prince then jumped down on Paul with the intention of killing Paul and doing to as quickly as possible, or else why did Prince not simply punch or kick Paul to unconsciousness?

Did Prince actually cause Paul's death? From our analysis, we know that Paul died while Prince's hands were around Paul's throat. We know this because of the attempt by Prince to hide Paul's body, showing that Paul was dead, as was proven above.

That being the case, it defies the laws of probability to believe that Paul actually died of any cause other than strangulation as he died at the exact moment that Prince was choking him. Accordingly, knowing Prince as I do (and as you have come to know him), I believe the logical deduction, beyond a reasonable doubt, from these facts is that Prince intentionally murdered Paul and that Paul died as a direct result of Prince strangling him.

END OF CHAPTER QUESTION

14. You have all the facts and I have made my case; what is your ruling; did Prince intentionally murder Paul?

Post your answer on www.breakingthecode.ca.

CHAPTER 20

DAMAGE CONTROL

The Immediate Aftermath of Madam Justice's Many Witless Comments

Undoing the injustice of Madam Justice

From the time of Madam Justice's unnecessary and insulting remarks from her imperial throne, my roommate has been attacked and has had multiple death threats. Some of those might have been deflected solely toward me without the nonsense that was spewed by Madam Justice to the thugs who were present in the courtroom to show their moral support for murder and to attempt to intimidate other witnesses and me.

Evidently, Madam Justice did not notice them glaring at me as she sat overlooking her empire trying to figure out exactly how to verbally punish me for what she seemingly believed to be my lifestyle choices.

There are actually some police who, recognizing what I had sacrificed in order to find justice for Paul and his family, called me a "hero." So, if Madam Justice couldn't find it in her to just say, "Thank you," I would have rather that she had said nothing at all, instead of questioning my motives and my forthrightness, and thereby publicly disrespecting me.

I am disgusted by Madam Justice's disregard or ignorance of what actually happens on the street to those who testify and with the arrogance she demonstrated by her total lack of any appreciation of the risks that I took to find justice for Paul and his family.

Madam Justice's unnecessary opinions, unsupported by the facts, were an affront to me and placed my roommate in added jeopardy, all because Madam Justice appeared to be too illogical to recognize the truth when she heard it, due to fact that she, not my roommate, not my roommate's family, not my roommate's friends, or my roommate's doctors or attorneys, and not even other justices in other courtrooms who pointed to me in open court and complimented me on being an excellent support for my roommate; no, none of those people, but only Madam Justice, found my roommate's relationship with me repugnant.

Anticipating the damage a seemingly feckless, clueless, and carefree Madam Justice had done to my roommate on the street, I immediately put up posters around the hood averring that I, and I alone, had worked with the police to put Prince in jail and that my roommate had no knowledge of what I had been doing. I did so in an effort to get ahead of the story and to put the heat back on me as it was my calling the police and my testimony and actions that helped to seal Prince's fate for him having committed a vicious murder.

My roommate had only been a minor character in a scenario that played out because Prince committed a murder, and her role had been forced upon her because she was compelled to testify, and even then, she could not testify as to what Prince said to me about his actions that night, about the crime scene, or even about exactly what had occurred in Paul's apartment, meaning that she was in court more as icing on the cake than as a critical witness. Therefore, on the street, after the trial, I sought to right the wrong done to my roommate by Madam Justice falsely disparaging my testimony.

With my roommate, still deep into her addiction, as I knew she would be, she bravely went about doing what she had to do to get her drugs. The inevitable harassment of her came as she was forced to fight and tolerate catcalls and threats, defending herself for the role she had played in the Prince matter, which although insignificant, had been mischaracterized on the street due to Madam Justice's many statements against me.

Following the trial and the oratory of Madam Justice at that trial, when I took my roommate to get her methadone in the mornings, she was often confronted by the idiots who obviously supported Prince's murder of Paul, idiots like Desiree Lemay and Crazy Beaudry (more on those two idiots later), challenging my roommate's right to be on the street, because she was subjected to screams of "rat," "goof," "fuck you," "you'll get yours," etc., with one fool being so daring as to follow us into the pharmacy to vent on and threaten her.

While my roommate testifying at all was obviously a key instigator in these verbal assaults, there can be no question that Madam Justice's ignorance or uncaring in not understanding the consequences to my roommate on the street due to Madam Justice pinpointing my roommate's testimony as credible and mine as not credible, played a large part in the frequency and intensity of these confrontations, designed to ostracize and intimidate my roommate.

Back to the pharmacy though, the reader might ask why we did not just switch the doctor whom my roommate saw and the pharmacy at which she drank her methadone. The answer to that is simple.

Were my roommate to have switched, she would have been regarded as running which would have been seen as weak and those showing weakness are more apt to be victimized. Besides, my roommate, still in her addiction, could not avoid those people at other times, so there would have been no point in switching.

Additionally, showing that kind of weakness could also be interpreted as a statement that my roommate thought that she was wrong for what she had done. I have always believed that when you do something you should own it. I am proud of my roommate that she took that lesson to heart and decided to stand her ground.

Finally, my roommate and I discussed switching pharmacies, but she decided that she also wanted to support me in what I had done and that one of the ways to support me was to not allow herself to be chased away, again making me proud.

My roommate and I got constant telephone threats from unknown numbers or we could be driving down a street far from the hood and suddenly hear "goof" being yelled from a passing car, or she could be walking down the street and some idiot bitch might yell "rat" from the back seat of a passing taxi.

Eventually I was able to convince my roommate to quit speaking defensively to others about what I had done and to give me ownership of it with a comment such as, "Hal didn't put Prince in jail, Prince put Prince in jail and Hal is proud of what he did; Hal is not from the street and he doesn't live by street rules." This tactic seemed to put the attention back on me where it belonged, which is exactly what I wanted.

Early on in the investigation, the police had suggested that I go into a witness protection program, but I declined for several reasons. Primary among those reasons was that I was not going to testify and then run like a coward (as I said earlier, I don't run), and I was not going to allow my roommate to face the music for my actions alone, even if it was only from the few idiots who wanted to show their support for animal torture, woman abuse, and murder.

At this point in time, things have settled down because everyone has heard about what I did and most give me, at least, a grudging respect, but there are still drama queens and haters out there proving their ignorance. Hating is what some people do to mask their own lack of accomplishments, lack of character, and lack of abilities, and there will always be haters, especially when there are drugs involved.

Just the other day as I was walking into the pharmacy to pick up my heart meds, some clown walked up to me and said, "I don't like you; you're a rat."

I responded with, "Can you give me a single reason why I would give a shit what you like or dislike?"

His response showed the logic by which these haters run their lives; he gave the following clever retort, "Fuck you," and then walked away.

I will give the guy props on one thing though; at least he had the parts to express his opinion directly to me rather than just talking smack behind my back as most other haters do.

CHAPTER 21

THEN CAME THE WANNABE, THE IDIOT, AND THE TIMES COLONIST

Friedrich Nietzsche: "**Whoever is dissatisfied with himself is continually ready for revenge.**"

Francis Bacon: "**Revenge is a kind of wild justice, which the more a man's nature runs to, the more ought law to weed it out.**"

George Bernard Shaw: "**Hatred is the coward's revenge for being intimidated.**"

Many times I would be talking with one of my friends while by a shelter or taking somebody to the doctor and my friend would point to somebody on the street and say, "That guy hates you."

I'd ask my friend who that guy is, and my friend would give me a name that I didn't recognize, and when looking at the guy, I didn't recognize his face either. We didn't know each other. Because he didn't know me, he could not have hated me; instead, he must have hated what I had done when I helped put Prince away and find justice for Paul and his family.

There are just some people whose life is so pathetic or who are so afraid of the truth about themselves that they have nothing better to do than to hate others. Below, are two of those doofusses.

Desiree Lemay

A Cowardly Schlub with a Weapon

A month after Prince's sentencing and Madam Justice's rant from the bench, a Desiree Lemay sneaked up to the driver's window of my car, immediately after my roommate had stepped into the car, and sprayed us both with bear mace, hitting me directly in the face and hitting my roommate with the overspray.

I quickly dialed 911 before I was completely incapacitated and we both hastily exited the vehicle to avoid further contact with the bear mace contaminated air, whereupon my roommate, in an act of caring and respect that belies Madam Justice's personal slant on the relationship of my roommate and me, immediately "assumed my back" as my roommate's vision had not yet entirely gone.

It was a scary moment for my roommate because she knew, at that particular time, that I had already survived six heart attacks and that the bear mace could have had potentially fatal effects on me if not promptly and properly treated.

In any event, the ambulance arrived, followed quickly by the police. We were treated by the ambulance attendants and released about forty minutes later to drive home; and Desiree Lemay, like the narrow minded coward she is, had disappeared into the wind along with the acrid smell of her weapon of choice.

Immediately prior to that attack when my roommate and I had just parked in front of the pharmacy and my roommate had exited the vehicle, Desiree Lemay had begun yelling at my roommate, calling her a fucking goof and telling her that she would get what she had coming to her for testifying against Wyatt (Prince). While I simply ignored the taunts as being proof of the idiocy of Lemay, my roommate being more emotional than I, yelled back at Lemay.

Thus, it is evident, while I received the brunt of the attack because it came through my window, that since Lemay waited for my roommate to return to the car and because my roommate was the one "called out" by Lemay, that my roommate was, at the very least, an intended victim. "Thank you, Madam Justice."

Again, I point out to Madam Justice, "Your unneeded rants have consequences, and in this instance, your words hurt the very person you thought you were protecting by openly displaying your contempt for me because of a relationship about which you did not have a single clue other than that you disapproved."

Blair Leslie Beaudry a.k.a.: Crazy
Another Spineless Hoodlum with a Weapon

At about 11:20 p.m. on June 26, 2012 (some sixteen months after Prince's conviction), I was sitting with a business associate in the parking lot at 3025 Douglas Street, maybe fifteen feet from my apartment door, Suite 107. My friend was examining a brochure that I had designed for his company when I saw "Crazy", beer in hand, walking across the parking lot in the direction of my friend's car and my suite.

A quick glance revealed to me that Crazy must be intentionally headed my way because there were no other people around us. I told my friend that we would have to talk later, that I needed to react to this threat. I considered it a threat because of some recent history between Crazy and me wherein he had been trying to intimidate my roommate, and because Crazy seemed to be walking with determination as my roommate, unaware, lay asleep within our unlocked suite. I immediately exited the vehicle and walked backward toward my suite because I wanted to keep my eye on Crazy.

Crazy quickly closed the distance that I had created between us, put his face, reeking of alcohol, up to mine, and said, "Bro, I heard some bad shit about you on the street; I heard that you put Wyatt away for murder."

I responded, "I helped put his ass away; he tortured my rabbit, threatened to fucking murder me, and he actually did murder someone."

Fortunately for me, I was on alert; after all, remember, I was face to fetid beer breath with a guy nicknamed "Crazy." I saw Crazy's face tense up a little as, feigning a "bro hug," he reached around my right shoulder with his left hand, firmly grasping the back of my neck, as if to draw me closer to him or impede me from pulling away. In the same moment, he reached for his right hand, pants pocket with his right hand, saying, "That kind of shit don't fly on the street bro."

I pulled back just as Crazy, obviously thinking he was some kind of avenging angel, was furtively extracting a stubby, yellow handled screwdriver from his too snug pants pocket. Because of the extreme tightness of Crazy's pants over his corpulent torso, the business end of the screwdriver got somewhat tangled on the edge of his pocket and fell to the cement walkway.

Crazy glanced quizzically at me as if wondering whether or not I had seen it, then looked at the ground to locate it (God forbid he should come at somebody like a man, mano-a-mano, without a weapon and without trickery), and in that moment, I was able to step backward the few feet to my door, which I then locked and immediately called 911.

While I was on the phone with the police, Crazy knocked on my door, saying that he wanted to talk. Through the door, I told him to go away as I had no desire to speak with him.

The police came within a few minutes and took a report, looked around a little for Crazy and put out a quick area alert (BOLO, be on the look out for) describing him and his clothing, but he was nowhere to be found. As with Desiree Lemay, another coward had fled, unwilling to stay to face the consequences of their actions.

The next day Crazy and I saw each other in my apartment building parking lot and Crazy said, "No hard feelings bro."

I replied, "No bro, we each have to take care of our own business in our own way." I guess Crazy thought that I was just going to wait for him to find some more liquid courage, something he found whenever he could steal, or otherwise scrape up, enough money for a twelve ouncer or a six pack of his favorite brew (whatever beer was closest to the front door and easiest to steal or whatever he could buy the cheapest).

I walked back into my apartment, and taking care of business in my way, called the police telling them where Crazy was. Perhaps his nickname should be "Stupid." After all, what did he think I was going to do, kiss and make up after he tried to shank me?

He should have known, especially after the Desiree Lemay incident, that I don't live by his ignorant code, and therefore, what the consequences would be if he messed with either my roommate or me, who incidentally, he had threatened earlier in the day.

Crazy was arrested, held for trial, and convicted of "assault with a weapon" on my testimony, which despite the fact that the defense tried to destroy my credibility by using Madam Justice's criticism of me against me, this particular judge found me to be "absolutely credible," even considering the fact that I obviously did not like Crazy, and moreover, even though I was totally focused on having the police look at Crazy as the only perpetrator.

As this was a trial by judge, not by jury, I shudder to think how Madam Justice Susan Griffin, considering her opinions in Prince's trial, might have regarded my testimony and what her judgment might have been had she been adjudicating the Crazy case.

Let us examine this incident right now to clear up this hatred psychology that led to Crazy's actions and show you haters what absolute fools you are and why you are not men (men actually control their own lives), but instead have surrendered total control of your lives to drugs, to a non-existent street code, and yes, even to me, the guy whom you profess to hate.

If I am able to evoke your anger and hatred through what I say or what I do, even though my words or actions have no direct effect on your life, who is in control of your emotions? That would be moi; I am in control; thank you for the power and control I have over you. All I have to do is ignore your "street rules", and I can use your hatred and anger to yank you around like a puppet. You are pathetic.

Your life is so out of control that it borders on absurd and you are so conditioned to giving away control that you do it almost as a Pavlovian response. First you give control to drugs by getting addicted to them and then allowing that addiction to define your actions; then you give control of how you should think and feel to some non-existent street code, allowing it to tell you who you should like, and even allowing it to drive you to hatred. Next, you allow that hatred to boil inside you and make you act like a fool, thinking that I might care if you dislike me.

I don't care what you haters think of me; I never did care, and I never will care. I don't bother to waste my time hating you back; in fact, at the rare times when I do think of you, I laugh at you or draw energy from your hatred as being hated by somebody of your lack of quality speaks better of me than might the praise of any three far more reputable individuals than you.

So, the facts are, when I do think of you, I am happy because I would rather be hated by you than loved by you, but most of the time you never cross my mind. I have better things to do with my life than to waste my time thinking about fools.

I am thankful that I don't live in your brain and that I actually control what I think, what I say, and what I do rather than allowing myself to be jerked around on the strings of hatred that control you like a marionette. The more you hate me; the more pathetic you appear to me and the less control you have over me and over yourself. That is part of what makes you such a loser in life, instead of making you a man.

I might show you the respect that any human should show every human, but as long as you waste your life being a hater and refuse to begin trying to take control of your own life, instead of trying to control the lives of others, I will never actually feel respect for you or ever think about you as anything other than a dope simple, violent fool as I watch you sew the seeds of your own destruction.

The irony here is that you attempt to control everybody with whom you have contact: your girlfriend, often through abuse; your other friends, often through lies about who you are or how "solid" you are; and those on the street, often through intimidation, and you do all this because you are trying to control everybody in your life to substitute for the fact that you can't even control your own life.

You will never control your life by trying to control what others think of you and how others behave. I control my own life because I don't allow what you might think of me to influence my decisions, because I compare my actions to what gives me self respect instead of to what might make others give me false respect, and because I am content enough with who I really am to tell others, as well as myself, the truth.

In a man's world, the truth is welcomed because it provides that man a tool by which to evaluate his actions, while in a hater's world the truth is something to be run from because it reveals a lack of character and accomplishments.

I think Glen Beck may have explained you haters as well as anybody when he wrote this of hating, "I was still searching for someone to blame for my suffering. I really wanted someone to transfer my hate to, so that I could stop hating myself."

CHAPTER 22

LOUISE DICKSON & THE TIMES COLONIST

The Ghana Daily Post Newspaper Editorial: **"An irresponsible press is no different from a mad dog on the prowl."**

Author's Note: After having been so offended about Dickson's article, the reader might reasonably ask why I am writing a book that could open old wounds.

1. *Dickson was wrong to publish her article because she was recklessly endangering my roommate and me, while publishing inaccurate and sensationalized information and identifying us.*
2. *It is my roommate's and my right to publish, not Dickson's, if we believe that there exist compelling reasons to do so.*
3. *With my roommate's permission, I am, herein, setting the record straight, not corrupting it, and I never used my roommate's name, as did Dickson.*
4. *In the years that have passed since Dickson's article, my roommate and I have reached an understanding with many of the people who initially had concerns about my actions.*
5. *Those people who still wish to be haters are entrenched in their positions already and the only hope to reach them is this book.*
6. *My roommate and I care about the people we have met on our journey and wish to reach out to them, and hopefully, encourage them to find sobriety and peace in their lives.*
7. *My roommate and I want to give abused women a way out of their prisons of terror.*
8. *I want to provide a roadmap to protect you from gangs and show you a way out of the drug world.*
9. *I have compelling evidence that suggests Prince is a psychotic killer and believe it important to get that message out.*

Following the bear mace attack referenced earlier, Desiree Lemay tried in vain to hide out from the police, a pointless maneuver as there is always somebody that will turn you in for twenty dollars just to be owed a small courtesy by the police. Accordingly, she was soon was arrested, and pled "Guilty" to assault with a weapon, obstructing justice, and various other charges.

Lemay appeared in front of a different judge than the judge in the Crazy trial. This judge, a judge who as with the judge in the Crazy trial, and unlike Madam Justice in Prince's murder trial, obviously understood the street and recognized the need to protect witnesses, even made a comment about the need to do so as he pronounced his sentenced.

Accordingly, in addition to time already served, Lemay was handed a further seven and one-half months in jail and banned from Vancouver Island after release (according to the Times Colonist, if you give it any credibility).

Lemay was not a particularly well liked person on the street and had, in my opinion, attacked my roommate and me in an attempt to garner "street creds". Lemay's sentencing took place some six months after Prince's murder trial, and due to Lemay's lack of popularity, her sentencing might have passed somewhat quietly, allowing things on the street to die down further regarding my roommate and me, were it not for a would-be Lois Lane, an elderly reporter for a local news rag, namely Louise Dickson and the Times Colonist.

Dickson, a well seasoned reporter for the Times Colonist newspaper, who apparently missed the point of the sentencing judge's lesson about protecting witnesses, and instead took a page out of Madam Justice's playbook on how to paint a target on witnesses' backs, wrote an inaccurate article that was published in the Times Colonist on August 19, 2012, about the Lemay conviction.

In that article, Dickson unnecessarily gave my roommate's complete name, and mine, and wrote about our roles in the Prince's murder trial, telling that I was paid for my role and that I had acted as an agent for the police, even exaggerating the amount I was paid.

The reporting done by Dickson included information that had never come up at Lemay's sentencing hearing about which Ms. Dickson reported, and had only come up some seven months earlier at the Prince murder trial. Why report on something that neither the Crown, nor the defense, felt relevant to the proceedings about which Ms. Dickson was reporting? I was stunned to read it in Ms. Dickson's article.

Dickson will probably tell anybody who might inquire, as she told me, that Prince's murder trial was a public trial, and therefore my roommate's role and my role were already known, so her article could cause no further damage. I say, "Poppycock." That is nothing more than an excuse to justify her recklessness. To demonstrate that fact, let's put her statement to the test of logic.

A newspaper is supposed to report "news". So, if our roles were already generally known, then that information was no longer news. Therefore, why include it in her "news" article when it gave the reader no greater understanding of the story and could only serve to further inflame the street and endanger us? The answer to that question, in my opinion, was to create sensationalism, and thereby, sell more newspapers.

I immediately sent an angry email to Dickson and to two of the Times Colonist editors, Bruce MacKenzie and Phil Jang, protesting that the use of our names was unneeded for the reader to understand the story, and adding that Dickson pointing out the fact I was paid in the Prince murder trial was inflammatory, especially when overstating the amount, and that the story could have been clearly reported without directing the street to our doorstep for more revenge; or for that matter, without even specifically mentioning the Prince trial.

When I received no reply from the editors, I sent out some four hundred and fifty emails to various journalistic schools, newspapers, television stations, radio stations, Crown Counsel Offices, and police departments. I wanted it understood by everyone what Dickson had done, because all that really needed to have been written to inform the public was something to the effect of, "Desiree Lemay was convicted of assault with a weapon and intimidation of the justice system after having bear maced two witnesses from a recent high profile criminal case here, blah, blah, blah." I was angry, and I still am.

Had I not been living out my senior years and spending my time continuing to try to help addicts into recovery, I might have been inclined to bring a lawsuit against Dickson and the Times Colonist. Let the record show that, as of the publication date of this book, neither my roommate, nor I, has received any apology. Additionally, there was no correction issued for the erroneous information, and perhaps speaking as eloquently as any fact about the apparent lack of any desire of the Times Colonist to "get it right," the article still remains on the internet, along with our names and the aforementioned incorrect information, and this is over two years later.

I firmly believe in a free press, but by that I mean a free and responsible press. I believe that if the courts are to expect that any witnesses come forward in the future and that the justice system remains intact, then something must be done to rein in reporters of Louise Dickson's ilk and editors who go ahead and publish anything their reporters write.

It has been many years since I authored a newspaper column, but in my day reporters spoke to the people about whom they were writing their articles and checked their facts before the editors agreed to go to print with their stories. Dickson made no effort to contact my roommate or me prior to her article, and failed to accurately check her facts.

Are witnesses now to be subjected to reporters for newspapers such as the Times Colonist using their names and sensationalizing stories with erroneous and dangerous information in order for those newspapers to compete with the internet? Must we be subjected to "yellow journalism" in search of the almighty dollar because a newspaper's revenues or profits might be flagging?

Publication of a Monday edition of the Times Colonist was not discontinued because it had too many readers or because it was selling too much advertising and making too much money.

Those in positions of authority, as is Madam Justice, and those who have jobs which are supposed to serve public interests, as does Louise Dickson, need to realize that their words have consequences and that they must weigh their desire to speak their mind or sensationalize a news story against the safety of those whom they supposedly serve. In my opinion, both Madam Justice and Louise Dickson failed in their respective duties in regard to the carelessness with which they spoke.

A Special Warning

To all justices and lawyers who might read this and wish to protect the justice system and witnesses, should you see Louise Dickson in the courtroom, I would like to respectfully suggest that you ask that a ban be imposed on her publishing the names of victims and/or witnesses.

If you would like to contact the Times Colonist, the editors thereof, or Louise Dickson about my opinions herein, you can do so at:

1. Dave Obee, Editor-in-Chief
   250-380-5201 dobee@timescolonist.com
2. Phil Jang, News Editor
   250-995-4443 pjang@timescolonist.com
3. Louise Dickson, Crime Reporter
   250-380-5211, ldickson@timescolonist.com

END OF CHAPTER QUESTION

15. Do you think Ms. Dickson's article should have included all the information it did?

Post your answer on www.breakingthecode.ca.

SECTION FOUR

UNDERSTANDING THE STREET

Khalil Gibran: "When you see a man led to prison say in your heart, mayhap he is escaping from a narrower prison and when you see a man drunken say in your heart, mayhap he sought escape from something still more unbeautiful."

CHAPTER 23

MY MESSAGE TO THE STREET

Khalil Gibran: **"You can muffle the drum, and you can loosen the strings of the lyre, but who shall command the skylark not to sing?"**

For the record, I understand that not all members of the street community are hard core drug users, thugs, user-dealers, or nonuser-dealers. This book is not meant to paint them with the same brush with which it paints the women abusers and the nonuser-dealers of drugs.

I also understand that there are people on the street who are there because of mental issues. It saddens me to see these people whose best conversations are often with themselves. For them, I sincerely wish our government had a solution, or would be willing to actually seek and fund a solution.

I further understand that there also people who are part of the street community who have chosen it as a way of life and are content with their choice. This book is not about them; they are exercising their freedoms in this great country and I wish them peace, happiness, and love. (I was a teenager in the hippie generation.)

To you users of hard core drugs, I hope that the harsh tone used herein is taken as a homily that encourages you to get help with your addictions and to find the happiness you seek. You should know that you will never find contentment at the business end of a crack pipe, a shard bowl, or a hypodermic needle. In fact, you cannot find it until you identify that from which you are running, and then stare it down and overcome it. I sincerely hope that you find the help, the courage, and the strength to do so.

Also, to you user-dealers of hard core drugs, despite some sobering words in this book, I understand the world in which you are caught and I empathize with your plight. A drug habit is a demanding task master.

I give you the same words of advice I give to users who are more able to support their habits without dealing. I also throw in the caution that you will get caught dealing and will go to jail, but on the bright side, perhaps finally to get clean.

To you nonuser-dealers, I will not call the police on you; I don't need to because karma, your greed, and your arrogance will get your ass busted. So instead, I'll just pray that karma drives a fast car.

As you rise to the top of your little pond, thinking you are a big shot because you are making a few dollars, remember that scum always rises to the top, until it is scooped up and disposed of.

To you women abusers and murderers, I will call the police if I am a witness to your depravities and I will testify against you.

To you women abusers, nonuser-dealers, and murderers I say, "May you reap what you sow; reap it baby, reap it."

To any of you drama seekers, backroom bitchers, and brain-dead idiots who think I was wrong to have turned in Prince and testify against him, think about this. After I did what I had to do, what was inarguably the only moral thing to do, after I helped put away that animal torturer, woman abuser and murderer, I put up posters around town telling what I had done and why I did it and then signed those posters.

Accordingly, if you think I was wrong, why don't you nut up or shut up; why don't you put up and sign your own posters explaining exactly why you believe that Prince should not be in prison and why you believe I was wrong to assist him in getting there? In fact, why don't you trade in some of your dope for a computer or a tablet and write a book about how wrong I was?

Do you have the parts to do that or are you too afraid that you will look to the general population like the fool you would be for espousing such an idiotic position? If you don't have the parts, and instead choose the cowardly path of Crazy or Lemay, coming at me or at my roommate in a sneak attack just as Prince attacked Paul, I will call the police, I will see you arrested and I will testify against you. Then I will laugh at you and mock you as I put your name in my second book.

You and your fucking code weren't doing anything about Paul's murder, so how did you expect Paul to get justice? I don't live by some idiotic, non-existent street code that seeks to victimize people and condones murder, and I WILL NOT BE YOUR VICTIM or underwrite your total lack of any moral scruples or brains.

I can just see one of you street code talking fools giving your teenage kid advice, *"Son, come here a minute; I know that I only see you once a year or so, but you're going to be a man soon and I need to teach you what is important in life. Listen up, no matter what happens out there, if it's rape, if it's murder, even if it's child molestation, no matter how wrong or evil it might be, you need to just walk away as though you don't know anything; don't say a word, because if you say anything to anybody who actually can, and will, do something about it, it would be very wrong of you. You must just allow any and all injustices to occur; this is the street code and living by the street code is how you become a man. Do you understand son?"*

Then you wonder why the next picture you see of your kid will be on his jail identification card instead of a graduation photo.

If you have a daughter instead, what do you say to her? *"Listen sweetie, I'm off to jail for a few years and in that time you will become a woman and find you a guy [Author's note: not a man]. That guy might beat you and abuse you. If he does, don't call the police to protect yourself; just take the beatings baby, and if you do decide to leave him and he finds you and beats you, you still can't call the police. Oh, and by the way, if he makes you sell your ass to support his dope habit, just go ahead and do it; that's what women are supposed to do. It's all about the street code, do you understand? Daddy loves you baby."*

Then, the next time you see your daughter again, if you get out of prison before her guy beats her to death, she'll likely have a surgically reconstructed face or tubes coming out of her to keep her breathing.

If that is what you teach to your kids, you're a fool; if it is not, then you're a damn hypocrite. [*Author's Note*: Ladies, if this is the same "would be wonderful father" with whom you are thinking of having a child, the next time he comes around I recommend that you take an aspirin………….. then place and hold it firmly between your knees.]

By the way Mr. Code Preacher, you don't have to teach children by talking to them; your actions teach them without words. So, what da fuck do you think your actions are teaching your kids with all your hating and street code bullshit?

Oh, I know, one of your dope buddies is going to protect your daughter. Wise up; your dope buddies are too busy doing their dope. Hell, when you get out, one of them will probably be pimping her to pay off her dope debt to him.

Lastly, it seems an all too common experience that somebody will have been talking to my roommate, not knowing who she is, and when the conversation ends, a third person would walk up to the individual who was talking to my roommate and say to that individual words to the effect of, "Do you know who you were just talking to? That was the woman who ratted Wyatt Prince."

Listen up you garbage-for-brains imbecilic haters; it was I who turned in Wyatt Prince, not my roommate. Do you get it yet? I turned him in; I'm glad I did, and I'd do again. There are certain things one does simply because they are morally correct. Do you need me to explain the word "morally" to you or perhaps to repeat the statement for you, or do you think you might finally be able to wrap your brain around it?

I only regret that Prince didn't stay out of jail long enough so his psycho ass could have strangled you too, because you are obviously another of the "I don't have a clue" class of fools who think murder is okay and who like to whisper your stupidity behind people's back. If lungs were made of brain matter, you would have suffocated a long time ago.

Besides, do you really think that the RCMP budgeted hundreds of thousands of dollars to an investigation just on my word or do you think that they first verified what I had to say with six or eight of your close bros? Hint: the RCMP doesn't do anything based on one person's word.

You haters are total idiots; rather than hating on me, you should be calling the police and telling them of other crimes that you know Prince committed, because frankly, when Prince gets out, and he will get out some day, you or somebody about whom you care might cross him.

Remember this also, when Prince does get out, he will get out feeling empowered because he expects you to fear him because he will be known as a killer, and therefore, feeling entitled because of the props that he will believe are due him because of having committed that murder. With that sense of empowerment and entitlement, he will believe that even the smallest slight of him, whether intentional or not, is a defiant act of disrespect of him and that he has the right, perhaps even the duty, to punish the offender.

Those feeling of empowerment and entitlement are exacerbated by the energy Prince will draw from you haters who send Prince and everybody else a message that murder and violence are okay. You are fools.

I protected you once, but I have no intention of making a career out of it. I know many of you are afraid of Prince and are happy he is gone. You are welcome.

CHAPTER 24

THE STREET CODE

Saint Ambrose: **"If you should live in Rome, live in the roman manner."**

Somewhere in all the talk of a "street code," people appear to have become confused and think of the "convict code" as the street code. This is because a lot of the code talkers (not the brave Native American code talkers of World War II) have done jail time, and due to the fact that the convict code is so heavily enforced in prison or jail, these former inmates want to transfer that code to the street for the feeling of security and control that it offers them and to allow them to victimize people without repercussions.

This appears to be the origin of the entire myth about there actually being a street code; that and Hollywood. What everyone needs to understand is that prisoners are confined when incarcerated and forced to be together twenty-four hours a day, seven days a week. Many of these prisoners are violent and need some basic simple rules, enforced by the overwhelming majority of other inmates, by which to operate or there would be constant fights, even riots.

In this environment, guards are heavily outnumbered and have no desire to wade into a situation wherein it is three to one or even ten to one or twenty to one against them, so they permit this convict code, as long as things do not get out of hand, because convict-to-convict peer pressure actually benefits in keeping things orderly.

On the street though, it is the police who are charged with keeping things orderly, not guards who have to rely on prisoners. Additionally, there are no B & E's to solve in jail, no bank robberies, no woman abuse, no crack shacks (although there is dope), no pedophilia happening, etc. On the street, people are free to come and go, free to hide and to live with whomever they want, wherever they want, and most importantly, free to talk to the police without everybody or anybody ever knowing.

Whenever you hear somebody preaching street code, you are likely hearing somebody who has done jail time and is trying to take the jail experience to the street. The street is not jail, never has been, and never will be; and in our society, outside of prison or jail, convicts are the minority, outnumbered a hundred to one by those who have never been to jail, and therefore, the street answers to society in general, not to a bunch of guys from Pod C at the local jail. Accordingly, the laws of society must rule the land, including the streets, not convicts with codes. Trying to enforce the convict code on the street makes about as much sense as trying to enforce hockey rules at a baseball game.

On the street, you rule your own life until you surrender that control to the courts by committing a chargeable offense or until you allow somebody to intimidate you enough that you believe that you must buy into an arbitrary and unenforceable street code that doesn't really exist and never will exist because nobody has you confined when you are on the street.

The majority of the street, just as in my case, will never accept the enforcement of a code that seeks to victimize them, nor should they. The street code preachers are outnumbered, outgunned. and out of jail, so they need to stop behaving as though they are still in jail and still in control or they will end up back in jail very quickly. Nobody can be successful trying to intimidate the world, especially if they are slinging dope and assuming all risks inherent in doing so.

CHAPTER 25

DOPE VERSUS THE CODE

John Grisham: "Shame was an emotion he had abandoned years earlier. Addicts know no shame. You disgrace yourself so many times you become immune to it."

Ralph Waldo Emerson: "The louder he talked of his honor, the faster we counted our spoons."

I say the louder he talks about how he would never steal from anybody, the tighter you should hold your money, your dope, your electronics and anything else of value. Remember, I used to buy used electronics, and I recall once buying the same phone three different times from three different people, all within a two-day period.

I also say that the louder he claims he would never talk to the cops, the quieter you should be. I can prove that many who Facebook how solid they are don't mean the same thing by "solid" as many might hope or think they mean.

They will remain nameless unless they do something to force me to publicly post my proof, as I have done before, and will happily do again. I know who many of you two-faced clowns are and if you want to fuck with me or with those about whom I care, I will play by my rules and I will fuck back, publicly with facts and photocopies.

ALWAYS bet on the dope and NEVER bet on the code. The street code of justice –although nonexistent as you will soon understand– is designed to intimidate and victimize women, the physically weak, and anybody who has been conned into believing it is real.

It is NOT a code of justice; it is an absolute guarantee of a total lack of justice of any kind. This supposed code seeks to turn any town into an Old West town wherein the fastest gun and most vicious individuals dominate. Think Billy the Kid or the Gene Hackman character in the movie The Quick and the Dead.

By the street code, if you are weaker than your victimizer, you cannot call the police, no matter what. The reason they beat on you is that they think they can get away with it because they think that you are too scared to call the police. You can prove them wrong with three numbers, 9-1-1.

If you are not allowed to call the police and get protection, then you will be that asshole's victim until that asshole overdoses and dies or until he goes to jail, which is what will happen to him, but maybe not before you take another few months, or longer, of beatings. Therefore, the justice will come in the end, but not from the street code, but from that asshole's lifestyle.

Listen up you everybody, including you wannabe gangstas, the hood is NOT La Cosa Nostra. In the Mafia they have a "no police" code, but they also have rules that are enforced by different levels of authority within the organization to protect the members of their organization and their women and families.

The basic rules are:

1. You must provide for your family.
2. Your family is untouchable in a dispute.
3. If you abuse any member of your family you must answer to the bosses.
4. You do not involve your family in your crime(s).
5. If you go to jail, your family will be provided for.
6. You do not kill another member without permission from the bosses.
7. You do not victimize anybody within the organization without permission from the bosses.

Compare that with the hood.

1. The hood is not an organization. Instead, it is a disparate bunch of desperate individuals running around and putting on airs, all in an effort to get high.
2. There are no bosses in the hood, only some assholes who are more brutal than other assholes.
3. There is no rule to provide for your family when you overdose or go to jail or just think smoking dope is more important than feeding your kid.
4. Girlfriends and wives of these hoodlum dealers often run their dope for them and are expected to take the fall (claim the dope as theirs) if their boyfriends are caught.
5. The victimizers will do whatever they can, including threatening your family to control you.
6. These victimizers seek nobody's permission. They are driven only by an insatiable appetite for dope or money.

The street code is a pimple on the ass of any area. If God wanted to give the world an enema, He would place it in the center of those fools who preach "street code."

What you call a street code is more of a "clown code" than anything else. What really exists is a constantly changing set of rules based on the situational morality of whoever has chosen to appoint himself/herself the "Almighty Protector of the Code," at any moment. In other words, when the situation involves them, their dope, or someone about whom they claim they care, what is right and what is wrong suddenly makes a dramatic change. It's just pure hypocrisy.

There is no oath of "Omerta" or anything else on the street; the only thing approaching a code is the old "I am out of dope so anything goes," or the old "Monty Hall," AKA: "Let's Make a Deal, Officer."

Here is an example of the victimization and pure idiocy of the precious street code in action. The other day, some fool fell asleep at one of the local shelters and got farmed for his dope and the guy who stole the dope started selling it, with none of his buyers having any possible way to know it was dope taken from the sleeping fool.

Is the buyer supposed to ask the seller if the dope is stolen or not. Even if the buyer did, does anybody think the seller is going to say, "Yup, I farmed it from butthead?"

What does the sleeping fool do when he wakes and discovers his dope gone? He decides that he knows who stole his dope because he asked around as to who was selling dope, but rather than confronting the guy whom he thinks stole it because the suspected thief is bigger than he, our sleeping moron tells the girls, not the guys, but the girls, that they now owe him for any dope they bought off the thief and if they don't pay, they will get their heads caved it.

It's just more drama, more bullshit, more victimization of women, and more sheer idiocy, and it happens continually. People get farmed every day and when it can't be determined who the thief was, the sleeping fool will randomly pick out a girl or some timid guy who was in the area and blame it on that individual. That's your idiot street code in action.

Perhaps you say that your bros would never steal your dope, then why do the cautious among you hoop it when you go to sleep? Why do you hide your money? Why do you only take either out of your pocket a little at a time?

You do it because you are afraid that your so called "bros" will rob your ass (figuratively speaking, of course, otherwise hooping it up your orifice would do no good). Hell, ninety percent of the time the people around you know better than you what you might have in your pocket at any given time because they watch you like a hawk when you have dope or money.

Why? They watch because they are looking for an opportunity. On more than one occasion, I have walked out of a store with a fresh pack of cigarettes and guys from, quite literally, a block away set upon me wanting to bum a smoke. They had been watching the store to see if anybody bought cigarettes. If they are watching for cigarettes, you know they are watching your dope and your money.

You are afraid of your bros for a reason. You are afraid because you know that there is no such thing as a "street code" or a "bro" when it comes to dope or money, and money isn't really money; it isn't really thought of as money, instead it is viewed as x amount of this narcotic and or that narcotic.

At various times, my friends have given me up to $25,000 cash to hold for them, and visa versa. We are bros, not bullshit artists looking for a fix or a victim. We don't live by some non-existent code; we live by something called "HONOR."

If you want to determine if you are acting with honor, ask yourself a couple of simple questions: "Are my actions in this dilemma absent any selfishness, absent any peer pressure, and absent any fear of being socially outcast by any individual or group? What would I hope somebody else would do when faced a similar decision or dilemma, and would I be unashamed to tell my maker and my family of my decision in this matter?"

Honor can never come from a code that only seeks to define your actions as those actions might relate to a limited set of circumstances; instead, it comes as a result of doing the right thing in any given moral dilemma; it comes from actually adhering to a set of moral principles rather than just giving them lip service. It especially does not come from a code that at its very core forces people to act against the best interests of victims and of society in general. I am not telling you what your moral code should be, only that you should have one by which you are content to live if you follow it.

Take your self-serving, delusional, daydream talk about a street code and put it where the sun don't shine; hoop it with your dope and your other gibberish. Your adherence to an ever-mutating, non-existent street code is nuttier than squirrel shit.

Now, let's examine some more drama from the dope world. If Sandy the Snatcher steals dope, or a phone, or whatever from Vince the Victim, then Alvin the Avenger will swoop in and attempt to get even with Sandy the Snatcher, but Alvin the Avenger doesn't give a crap about Vince the Victim. No, Alvin the Avenger just wants whatever was taken to keep for himself and uses the "Vince the Victim is my bro" line as an excuse to victimize somebody who had already victimized Vince the Victim. Hell, Alvin the Avenger might even dislike Vince the Victim.

It's all a bunch of posturing. Everybody is looking for excuses to rob somebody. Half the time Vince the Victim was making up bullshit that Sandy the Snatcher robbed him, maybe because Vince the Victim smoked somebody else's dope and was trying to create a story to avoid getting a beating himself.

It gets more vicious, though, for as soon as a dealer with a place to live is arrested, some addicts will break into that individual's home and tear through it, taking his/her belongings and hoping to find drugs or money that the police missed. Don't you wonder how many dealers have been turned in just to create that opportunity? It's dog eat dog and everybody barks.

Often times a person gets robbed just because that person has money or dope. Some of the robber(s) feel that they have to make up an excuse for themselves as to why they are going to commit the robbery. That's easy though, all drug addicts lie to themselves. Incidentally, that's why Paul died. Three guys high on drugs found an excuse to rob somebody whom they knew had money. People get robbed with machetes or bear spray, beaten, and worse, simply because some thugs want to rob or hurt somebody.

This is your code? It's bullshit; there is no code; there is only a raggle-taggle bunch of addicts, spouting whatever crap they think will give them an excuse to rob or hurt whomever their victim of choice might be on any given day. Then you have the really dangerous ones who don't need an excuse. They just rob you because they can never experience any self-shame.

When I was on the witness stand in the Prince trial, Prince's attorney, in an effort to discredit me with the jury, accused me of buying stolen electronics off the street, along with other alleged misdeeds, all the while with law enforcement in the room. Where do you think the defense attorney came up with his questions? The answer is obvious. Prince accused me of doing those things.

So, what happened to the precious code? Is having your paid mouthpiece accusing somebody, by proxy, any different than you ratting? That must be an exception to code, huh? Does the code read, "Don't be the first to rat," or does it read, "Don't rat?" Tricked you, it doesn't read anything because there is no code. Remember? It's all bullshit.

You should all be happy that there is no code. You should be happy because without a code you cannot be victimized because you can call the cops to end the victimization.

I know, I know, there are some of you will say, "If somebody killed my bro or a member of my family, I'd handle it myself." You are either a hypocrite, or an idiot, or both.

Why did nobody avenge Paul's death then? Are you trying to tell me that nobody out there smoked Paul's dope with him, that Paul was nobody's "bro" and that none of you ever called him "bro" so he would piece you off?

Was that murder okay with you? What would you do if Davie the Diddler was victimizing some children? If murder is okay, what about other stains on society?

What about the degenerate in Chapter 1 who was defiling and victimizing the fifteen year old child of God who was given a heroin overdose? Pedophilia must be okay because all you people who knew what was happening just sat there with your rigs in whatever artery you could still find and let that obscenity occur and continue.

I'm choking back tears, overwhelmed by the warmth of that lesson; not! I'm disgusted by all your talk of a street code. Where do you draw a line in the sand? What about robbing senior citizens, where is your deal breaker?

The truth is that dope and the fear of being shunned by the street have robbed you of any morals or code which you might have had. You betray yourself daily.

Because you now know the hood is not an organization and there exists no code, let me pose another question, "Do you have a code"?

If you had a personal code, you would have a line in the sand. What is that line? Is it that you knew the victim and that makes it not okay, is it that you know the victimizer so that makes it okay, or is it that you dislike the victimizer, so fuck him, or is it because your sorry ass is too scared of the victimizer to do the right thing?

What will you allow to happen without you putting an end to it by calling the police or are you one of those non-forward thinking idiots who say that you would handle it yourself? Well, you didn't handle it with Paul; you left it to me to avenge Paul and nobody has been arrested for the fifteen year old girl. Instead, you just did another fix, pushed your pipe a few more times, and kept moving forward with your addiction and your street code. I had your back though.

Let's examine this "I will handle it myself" stupidity anyway; let's pretend that you actually intend to do something rather than beak off and chase your dope. Somebody kills Alvin the Avenger's real brother, putting a hole in Alvin's family. Alvin, true to his name, wants to avenge that killing. Consequently, Alvin kills the dude who killed his brother, and because

Alvin was the obvious suspect, the Crown prosecutes Alvin and Alvin is sentenced to x number of years in jail.

Now, not only is Alvin's family without Alvin's brother, they are also without Alvin. Thus, in order to right the wrong of the murderer destroying Alvin's family, Alvin destroyed his own family even more by committing a murder himself. Now, not only will Alvin's kids grow up without an uncle, but also without a father. As I said, they don't call it dope because it makes you smart.

You people who consider yourself members of the hood are actually members of nothing. The hood is an area, not an organization, not a religion, nor even a political faction. You cannot belong to something that does not exist. The hood is as fictional an organization as the street code is a code.

You are probably doing drugs because you somehow felt unaccepted as a child or because of some failure that stole your self-respect, and you turned to dope to run from that lack of acceptance or from that failure. I get it; drugs for you, at least initially, were probably part escape and part rebellion, but what have they become now?

The truth is that for that part of you that wants acceptance, you find comfort in believing that there is an organization and a code, that you are part of a group and that you are loved, respected, and protected by that group and its code. It's not true and it never will be true.

It will never be true because you have joined nothing; you are just a lone individual who is trying to support a drug habit, either to stay high so you can keep on running from yourself or to keep from getting down sick. You are doing this because somewhere along your journey with drugs, the drugs became your prison instead of your escape. That's what always happens with drugs.

That guy across the street who gives you a friendly nod might be the same person who will be planning to rob you if you ever do have a few dollars.

Have you ever owed somebody $20 when he is down sick? What happened to the friendship then? It's, "Give me my money now or I will kick your ass." When you sell somebody dope or piece him off, he only got a pebble, but when he gives you a pebble, he claims it was a boulder. Friendships among addicts are about dope and everybody loves the guy with the dope or the money until the dope is gone or the money spent, then they love somebody else who has dope or money.

Set aside your pretenses for a minute and look deep into your soul and say that you are the exception, that you have never stolen dope from a comrade while he was on the nod, or while he was looking away. Have you never grabbed a five dollar bill or a three dollar hoot? It's bullshit if you are addicted and tell me that you haven't.

We all know that when somebody goes down from an overdose that there will be somebody else who will grab the unfortunate soul's dope or money, and sometimes even other possessions. There's a damn lineup.

When did stealing from your bros become okay? I'll tell you when; it became okay when you lowered your moral standards to the point that your dope habit was more important than any sense of personal honor.

There is no street code, but that doesn't mean that you have to live without some sort of personal code that defines what you will not do, more than it defines what you will do. The problem is that at some point, if you are addicted, you will have no personal code. Your addiction will steal it just as it steals everything else in your life.

If you are without a code, you are adrift in a cruel ocean whose whirlpools suck you in and under and steal your beliefs, your hopes, your life, and your psyche. Therefore, if you are doing drugs, you will end up unrecognizable to yourself, a mere shadow of who you were.

A person without a code is a person with dead eyes, a dead conscience, and a dead future. You know what I'm talking about here; you have watched many who were once your friends change to the point that you wonder what you were thinking when you befriended them or allowed them to befriend you.

Many of the people you know are now looking at you with the same wonderment with which you now look at others. The sad irony here is that all of you are correct in your assessments.

Somewhere in a comic book, or a novel, or a movie, or a TV show, or from your parents, or from whomever or whatever, you saw a little spark of something that looked right to you or that seemed morally correct at that time. Seize that item, drink it in, and make it the start of your code. Start changing your life.

What is it that drives your fear? Are you afraid of failure, or does success scare you more? Think about it. What keeps you using drugs?

You people on the street talk about respect. Let me break respect down for you again. Giving somebody the absolute truth is giving him/her absolute respect. Each lie tears at the fabric of respect.

Therefore, I give you absolute respect because I give you absolute truth. You don't even give yourself respect because you lie to yourself all the time. How can you give somebody else respect; how can you give what you don't have?

Give yourself truth and you will begin to learn how to respect yourself. Take the spark of that memory from wherever it came and add self-truth to it and you have started a journey out of the hell you have created for yourself.

Do you have the guts or do you still want to lie to yourself every day as you anesthetize yourself from your self-imposed misery with your drug(s) of choice? Crosby, Stills, Nash, and Young had an insightful line in one of their songs; it said, "The truth you're running from is so small, but it's bigger than the promise of a coming day."

From what truth are you running? Do you have the guts to face it or would you prefer to end up dead in a gutter or an alley somewhere, to be one of the two people from the downtown core who are buried every week because of drug-related deaths?

That's right. Just in our little city alone, two of your friends die every week because of drugs. For how long do you think you can dodge the bullet? Look around you. More than one hundred of your friends will be dead in the next year.

Studies have shown that once you start doing your drugs intravenously, that your life expectancy is 12 to 17 years. How many years do you have left? Are you living on borrowed time yet?

Man up or woman up and face your life; and remember, it is your life, so nobody else can face it for you. The truth is that you do not get high anymore, not like when you started doing drugs. Instead, now, when things are good, you just subsist; when they are not good, you get down sick or do some stupid crime that eventually sends you to jail. This is the hell that you have created for yourself.

On the street, your nights are the same as your days. You get little sleep, sometimes bob and sway from that lack of sleep, and all the while try to support your drug habit with a mind that is increasingly paranoid and irrational and a body that refuses to function normally due to the ravages of drugs and sleep deprivation.

You are not in a groove; you are in a rut, a rut that just keeps getting deeper as you run back and forth desperate for more drugs to feed your ever-growing habit while your body falls apart, your teeth rot, and all definition of who you are is sucked out of your face, out of your heart, and out of your soul.

Instead of attempting to manage your addictions, though, you keep sinking deeper and deeper into them as it takes an ever-increasing amount to satisfy your cravings and/or stay unsick from heroin withdrawal. You build up your need for heroin each time you have money and when the money disappears, you get sick.

The only thing that ever slows the growth of your addiction is running out of money; and you will always run out of money or go to jail. There will never be a point where you can consistently manage your addictions and support your habit because every time you think that you may have enough money, you do more dope and increase your habit. I have watched numerous individuals go through $25,000 to $30,000 in a matter of a few days or a week. You have seen it, too.

Whenever I think of drug addicts, I always think of an alleged Axel Rose interview from years ago. The interviewer supposedly told Axel that the word was out that Axel had a dope problem and asked Axel if it was true. Axel supposedly responded with words to the effect of, "I don't have a dope problem; I have a dope habit. I can afford all the dope I want; I'm filthy rich. The only ones who have a dope problem are the ones who are addicted and can't afford their dope."

Well, you ain't Axel Rose and even Axel ended up going into rehab. Stand up, wise up, and man up; stop the idiocy. Try rehab. It won't work if you don't try it, and when you fail at it, do it again, and again, if necessary. You haven't lost until you quit trying.

Get clean! Nike had a slogan that said, "Just do it." Have you ever thought about what that slogan means? It means, don't just think about it; don't just talk about; don't just plan on doing it, or even just try to do it. It means, just do it!

CHAPTER 26

IT'S CALLED HONOR

Khalil Gibran: "Man struggles to find life outside himself, unaware that the life he is seeking is within him."

Socrates: "The greatest way to live with honor in this world is to be what we pretend to be."

I was born in Canada, but spent my formative years, from about age eight to fourteen, growing up in Texas, the Lone Star state, with a father who was Texan through and through. Texas is more like its own country than it is like one of the other forty-nine U.S. states.

I grew up with both golf and guns, learning how to hit the ball by age eight and how to shoot straight with a rifle or a handgun by age ten. Guns are part of the culture in Texas and even in those tender years I owned a few.

There is something else that is part of the culture in Texas too; we spelled it h-o-n-o-r when I lived down there; up here we spell it h-o-n-o-u-r, but it doesn't make any difference how you spell it; it means the same thing. It means that you have a few rules in your life that are sacrosanct, rules that would have been beaten into you, if necessary. Those were the days of "spare the rod and spoil the child" and neither my brother, nor I, was ever spoiled.

In Texas, contrary to the Hollywood image, they don't care much about the Lone Star belt buckles, the Levi blue jeans, the Tony Lama boots, or the Stetson ten-gallon hats; that every Texan wears those things is fiction. To be sure, if you go to Texas you will see your share of all of the above attire, but I never saw my father wearing any of those things and he was more of a man than any I have met.

That's because it's not about what you wear down there; the clothes do not make a person a Texan. It's about what you do; it's honor that defines a Texan just as it is honor that defines a man. Everybody can dress as if they are a Texan or pretend they are a man, but few can live a life that matches their pretenses.

So, forget the situational ethics of a street code, forget the threats, and forget being a victimizer. Forget the hatred that ruins your day more than it bothers the individuals(s) upon whom you are hating, forget the lies to yourself and others, lies which fool nobody, and forget hitting or disrespecting women.

Instead, stop just talking the talk and start walking the walk and grab yourself a fist full of honor, and in doing so; adopt a simple, personal code of honor, be true to yourself and that code, and thereby change your life and your legacy.

To have honor, one has to live by a few uncomplicated rules:

1. Don't lie. Every lie eats at the fabric of your manhood and leads to more lies and eventually ends in shame.

2. Always do as you say you will do, making your word your bond.
3. Do not tolerate victimization or injustice if it is within your ability to change it.
4. Never speak or act disrespectfully to a woman.
5. Take ownership of your actions.

If you couldn't do those simple things, then you needed to get the hell out of Texas and not call yourself a man. It was, and is, that simple.

To find honor, always judge yourself by this code to see if you are a man. If you don't qualify, then change your behaviors, not your code. When you change your behaviors, you are not just changing how people see you, which in the long run doesn't mean a damn thing anyhow, because it is you who makes you happy, not those other people.

The important thing you will be changing is how you see yourself, which will ultimately change who you are and bring contentment and tranquility to your life. Once you have changed who you are, your list of friends will change also; and that is good, for as humans, we tend to become like our friends, so that change is needed.

As you are shedding those who don't measure up to the standard of actually being a man, remember that the character of a man is better judged by his list of enemies than by his list of friends. So quit worrying about who likes you, and instead, do what you need to do to become your own friend, and make the right enemies instead of the wrong friends.

Until you do this, until you can look in the mirror and honestly like and respect yourself, you will spend your life being less than a man because you will spend your life running from yourself, and nobody is that fast, not you, not anybody.

SECTIONFIVE

Abuse, character (or lack thereof), legacies, fighting the fight, and understanding the drug business

The drug business is the only business in the world in which success is dependent on the number of lives and families you are able to destroy.

Sophocles (Circa 460 BC): "**More men come to doom through dirty profits than are kept by them.**"

CHAPTER 27

POLICE AND THEIR ROLE IN THE HOOD

Police perform a vital service for every member of society, including you and your family. What do you do for your family or for society?

Police are not your enemy; drugs and gangs are your enemy. You are more your own enemy than police.

Police are your friends when you really need a friend and that is the best kind of friend to have.

Ralph Waldo Emerson: "The reward of a thing well done is having done it."

Unknown Author: "The enemy of my enemy is my friend."

The other day I took one of the working girls to lunch. This is a relatively regular occurrence with me because I enjoy just talking with them, learning about their pasts and about their aspirations for their future, or just sitting silent with them if that is their comfort zone.

It is nice to get to know them as real people and let them know that I will try to be there for them when they are ready to quit drugs and to start earnestly pursuing their hopes and dreams.

Anyhow, she and I were chatting – actually, I was listening and she was doing all the chatting – about the recent arrest of a dealer who had wanted to take this particular lady to another city to work, instead of her working here. She wisely declined. Telling me about why she had declined – I did not ask – she gave the following soliloquy,

"He must have thought I was crazy to want to go over there and be pimped out, spend weeks flat on my back and get beaten by him and his friends."

"I like my safe little city; I can walk down any street at any hour and feel safe. The cops watch out for me and the other girls; there are no pimps here, no gangs; I can just do my thing until I am ready to get clean. Why would I leave here? This is the best place in Canada."

"I like the cops and I feel safe because I know they care. There are some asshole cops, but there are assholes everywhere. People need to quit calling them pigs or cussing them; they're just doing a job."

"[Name withheld for privacy] had a bad date the other day; the guy took her to his hotel room, smacked her around, demanded that she give him a blow job, and punched her in the head while she was doing it. She escaped and was hurt and crying, but would not call the cops because she did not want to be a rat. Fuck, that's not being a rat; that's refusing to be a victim."

Bravo! This lady absolutely gets it and was spot on with everything that she said.

You need to wake up and understand that the peace and safety you experience here is a direct result of the police department(s) keeping the gangs and the pimps out of the area.

Let me break it down for you like this:

1. To you ladies, read the quote from the lady with whom I had lunch and realize that you get the same protections as she. Nobody is throwing you on a mattress in the backroom and holding you there against your will to provide sexual services to

whomever your captor might desire.

2. Also to you ladies, if you get a bad date, you can call the police and they will treat you with respect, take your complaint seriously, and even try to protect your girlfriends from your predator so those girlfriends do not suffer the same fate as you. CALL THEM, I BEG YOU.

3. To you dealers, nobody is threatening you, beating you, stabbing you or shooting you, or telling you that you are not allowed to work at this corner or that corner unless you buy your dope from them.

4. To you users, male and female, nobody is threatening you or beating you if you don't buy your dope from them.

The reason for this is that the police are protecting you. They keep the gangs out and keep you safe. It is that simple; you need to understand why you live in a safe, little city.

Do you think that happens by accident? Not only no, but hell no. It happens by vigilance, by leadership, by police having a plan, by adhering to that plan, and by the cops working together as a team and focusing their resources and efforts on protecting the citizens, of which you are one.

If for no other reason than that, the next time a cop car rolls by you, you should flash a quick smile, or give a slight nod or a friendly wave, and if some idiot challenges you for doing so, just break it down to that fool the way I have broken it down here. Tell that fool who wants to diss you that he is able to do so because of the blanket of protection afforded him by the police.

Does this mean that all cops are nice people? Again, "Not only no, but hell no." Just as the lady said, there are some jerk cops and I have met a few of them, just like there are jerk garbage collectors or jerk lawyers.

Some of you guys are jerks; there are jerks in every profession, every job, and every walk of life. And, just like the rest of society, cops are a cross section of the people, with most, at least, being ok individuals, and some being really great people. I had the privilege of working with a few of the really great ones on Paul's murder, on Crazy's attack, and on the Lemay attack, and still have their numbers in my phone book.

So you think cops are cowards because they often come in the middle of the night or they come in large numbers? If that is what you think, you are a fool.

They often come in the middle of the night to surprise you. If they can catch you off guard, there is a much lesser chance that you will do anything stupid, and if you do nothing stupid, then nobody will be hurt, not any of them, and not you. They surprise you to protect you and to protect them. Do you get it?

Why do they come in large numbers? They do it to protect you and them through intimidation. If you are intimidated, then there is less chance that you will do something stupid and if you do nothing stupid, then.............. Are you starting to see a pattern here?

Do you hate the cops because they arrest you? Let's break that down right now. Assuming you're a criminal of some nature, then you have chosen to make committing crimes your job. It is the job of the police to bust your ass for doing your crimes. It's that simple.

You're the one who wanted a seat at the big table, but then didn't play well enough to keep your seat, so who is really at fault for you being arrested? Take ownership of your actions and stop blaming others because you fucked up.

Those of you who are arrested and who then start ranting about how you hate the pigs, what you are really doing is whining because they were smarter than you. When I was raised in sports, we were not happy about losing to another team, but our coaches taught us to shake our opponent's hand and resolve within ourselves to play a better and smarter game the next time.

If you sit on the curb, hands cuffed behind you as you make snorting noises or hurl your invective ridden insults at the cops, you are a whining, sniveling idiot. With each snort, with each foul word, and with each taunt, you are telling the cops that you hate them for being smarter than you, and you think that is going to get under their skin?

Hell no; it will only make them laugh at you and feel happier that they busted your dumb ass. I'm not suggesting that you go shake their hands, (you can't anyhow because you are the fool with your hands cuffed behind your back), but I am telling you that you might look more like a man if you just shut up.

What do you think the other team would have been doing if our coach had told us, after losing a game, to begin yelling at that team? They would have gone to the locker room laughing at us and thinking what losers we were. Then they would have resolved to kick our asses even harder the next time we met. When you sit on the curb acting like a fool, the people from the street who have even half a brain are quietly laughing at you as you paint a target on your back because you make yourself so much fun to arrest.

So, you still think you're a smart guy, huh? Then why in the hell is some uniform with a hand spread atop your head helping you into a paddy wagon while you are wearing the bracelets of stupidity if you're so smart? Can you explain that one, fool?

CHAPTER 28

THE DRUG BUSINESS

One definition of insanity is continually doing the same thing and expecting a different outcome.

So, you want to be a dope dealer, then you are an idiot. You are entering a game at which you are guaranteed that you will go to jail. It is that simple.

Almost everything I see dealers do is antithetical to common sense, guaranteeing they will get caught, even without the cops targeting them.

Having a Facebook page showing all your connections with other dealers and users and bragging on that page about how you would never rat is probably not your best move if you want to stay on the "down low". News flash: cops can read and actually know how to access your Facebook page. If you had another brain you'd be a half wit.

If you keep doing what you've always done, you'll always get what you always got.

King James Bible, Proverbs 14:16: "A wise man feareth, and departeth from evil: but the fool rageth, and is confident."

<u>User-Dealers</u>

The facts are that if you choose the dope business you have chosen a game at which YOU WILL EVENTUALLY LOSE unless you have a perfect record. If you are less than perfect, your ass will get arrested at some point and you will go to jail. In other words, you have chosen a fool's game.

The proof of this is that if you are dumb enough to get into, and stay in, the dope business, with all the resources police put toward it, then you are too stupid to have the perfect record needed to stay out of jail.

Do you know any dealers who have been slinging for a year or more who have never been to jail or who are not currently facing charges? What makes you think you will do better than they did?

Most dealers are serving life sentences, but on the installment plan. Let us look at what stands between your perfect record and your installment plan.

Do you intend to deal heroin? If yes, what do you think is going to happen when you won't front your customer a point of down? Do you think he/she will be angry after they have been spending their money with you for x number of days/weeks/months? What will they do if they get dope sick and a cop offers them $40 to go buy from you?

Ok, so not fronting is not an option. Therefore, you front them, and now, because they owe you and don't owe some other dealer, they go to that other dealer because they don't want to spend their money with you and get half of the amount of dope they would have gotten had they gone to the other dealer.

Fine, now you are going to threaten them to get your money back. Of course, threatening them won't bring them back as a customer. So you lost the customer when you fronted him/her and you would have lost him/her as a customer if you had refused to front. So, you were damned if you did and damned if you didn't. That's the dope business; you are always damned.

Let us suppose that your threats actually scare your customers; what will they do? They might pay you and they might not, but either way, when the cops come to them looking for a name or when they get jammed up and need to give a name to get out of their problem, what name do you think will come tripping off their tongues?

Accordingly, whether you front the heroin or not, you have created an addict who has no use for you, and an addict who has no use for you is a liability. So, even if you were not on the police radar before, you soon will be. You will be on your way to jail soon because you have to multiply that one example by every heroin addict to whom you sell.

Because dealing heroin is out because down sick addicts are unpredictable, what about slinging cocaine? You have the same problems with fronting versus not fronting, but you do avoid the dope sick addict.

The problem for you here is that if you don't sell heroin, the only people who will come to you are those who don't want heroin when they meet you. Therefore, you will, at most, be dealing with only 20% of the potential client base, making your business difficult to grow.

Moreover, now you are of no use to some 80% of the addicts. That is a lot of addicts whom you expect not to put a bounty on your ass because they are in a jam or because some cop offers them $40, especially when they have no need of your services.

Stick a fork in you, you are done like dinner. It is not a matter of "if" you will be caught and go to jail, it is simply a matter of "when." Therefore, slinging only cocaine is out.

That brings us to crystal meth. Again, you have the same fronting issues, while avoiding dope sick issues, but you are in just as much trouble as with either cocaine or heroin because people who use crystal meth are far more prone to violence, plus you are of no use to any of those who do not use crystal meth.

Let us take everything a step further and suppose that you are going to sell all of the above or any of the above and that you will beat the crap out of anybody who owes you money. Then, you will develop a reputation for being dangerous, limiting the number of people who will deal with you, giving your beating victims real reasons to turn you in; and because you are dangerous, bringing on intense police attention. Bye, I'll see you when you get out of jail.

You need to understand that if you have been slinging for a month or more, the cops probably have your name; have your phone number; know where you live, assuming you are not homeless; know who your customers are; and know your meeting places. Why aren't you in jail yet? Because they haven't gotten around to you yet; but be patient, they will.

How do you avoid "buy and bust" operations of the police wherein they watch known drug addicts and photograph them buying dope or actually get an undercover cop to pose as an addict and buy from you, or just get an addict to buy from you?

I can tell you from experience that during the Prince investigation, there came a time wherein the cops had to follow me on foot. I knew they were there, but I couldn't tell the cops from the rest of the people on the street. The only way you can be assured that you won't get caught in a buy and bust operation or not get photographed dealing is to never leave your house with dope, or instead, to send out a runner with dope, but that runner might talk if he/she is caught.

What do you do to protect yourself from your competition, the other dealer who figures that if you are not slinging he will have more custies to serve? In this guy's head, he also gains another way because he hopes the cops will cut him a break because he turned you in; they won't, but at least he will keep them busy with your ass.

Do you use a runner? What do you do if your runner pinches the bag? The runner goes out with a delivery and pinches. The customer calls you and says, "Hey the bag was short or the rock was small?" The runner now says, "I didn't pinch." Is the customer lying or is the runner lying?

If the runner is lying, then you have a pissed off customer who has no use for you, and we all know now where that goes. How can you know who is the liar?

I understand, you can use a runner who doesn't do dope, but how do you know that the runner is not pinching a little off each delivery until he/she has enough dope to sell a twenty bag here or there in order to make a few extra dollars?

Your runner is a criminal, right? So, would it be above her/him to pinch and sell? You lose either way.

So, you can't use a runner and you can't sell on the street and you won't sell to anybody you haven't known for x amount of time and you will only sell behind the closed door of your crib and everything will be cool, right? WRONG!

You still have the fronting problem; and now, all the traffic to your door causes your neighbors to have concerns. Oops. Further, you don't know who is following who to your house, whether they are being watched by cops this trip or on a future trip or whether the cops actually gave them money to buy off you.

Moreover, you don't know who might be planning to rob you because everything that happens will be indoors, unseen from the street. Remember Prince robbed and murdered Paul, and Paul wasn't even a dealer, but it probably would not have happened in an open area.

I know, I know. You will have a few weapons around to deal with any robbers. Great plan! Then, when the cops kick in your door, which they will at some point, you will also have a weapons charge or two against you.

You think that you have all those problems worked out and nobody would ever consider ratting you out? You forgot about your worst enemy, you.

You or your runner leave some buyer hanging around on a street corner for thirty minutes or longer based on a half a dozen "I'll be there in five minutes" promises. Then, anybody driving by who has half a brain knows that person is waiting for the dope man, and you wonder how the cops got onto you, perhaps you even blame your custie for your problems, calling him or her a rat.

Sometimes, in the brilliance brought about by dope use, you stack up two or three buyers on the same corner, thinking the store owner, the apartment dweller, or the homeowner will not call police, while you sit on your couch or floor teching on your bike or on whatever might be the instrument drawing your attention at the moment.

In the meantime, your custies might be stumbling around sleep deprived or dressed in black clothes with their hoodies pulled over their heads in the middle of a warm summer day, wearing baggie pants falling down so low that they are exposing their ass crack. Other times they will get agitated and start stomping and cussing, making a scene.

I have witnessed hundreds of deals taking place on busy street corners with the buyer and the seller exchanging money for dope with both the money and dope openly visible to every passerby. What are you thinking?

Let me score you a break here, loud open discussions about drugs, the open act of scoring drugs, belligerent behavior in public, standing around for twenty minutes on street corners checking your watch every two minutes, or flailing through your backpack or purse might be ordinary behaviors to those involved with drugs. To the general public they are not ordinary behaviors and people actually get offended or intimidated and call the police.

Okay, you can't meet your custies or have your runner meet your custies on an openly busy street, and you don't want the meet to happen in a drug area because of the heat that brings. Instead, you pick an alleyway somewhere. What do you imagine people think is happening when they see somebody standing around an alley? Do you figure they think that person is up to anything worthwhile? Somebody calls the cops and you'll be getting your mail in jail if anybody actually writes you.

All the above does not count the times that you shit your own bed, staying up for days smoking all your product and finally falling asleep, and waking up later down sick with no money and no dope. It is an extremely rare individual who can actually maintain a dope habit and a dope business, both. We all know of several user-dealers who have fallen asleep at a stop light, only to be awakened by the cops.

There are two problems with being a user-dealer; those problems are you and your customers. Then add the general citizenry and the police into the mix and, "See ya, wouldn't wanta be ya," you are headed to jail.

When you do come out of jail, you come out broke and needing to front in order to get started again or depending on a welfare cheque to achieve re-supply. Thus, you start behind the eight ball (no pun intended) and still have to deal with all the problems above, again.

Do you still want to be a dealer? If so, the best you can hope for is that when you are caught few times that you get clean in jail, take some courses, and find a job with some sort of future when you get out. Otherwise, you will be right back in because the cops will focus attention on you as you are a dealer fresh out of jail. It's real simple, just as I said before, if you keep doing what you've always done, you'll always get what you always got.

Nonuser-Dealers

If you are slinging and not supporting a habit, it means that you are slinging for pure greed, and when you are caught, which you will be, the judge is more likely to throw the book at you because you have made a conscious decision to kill people and to destroy families simply so you can have a few more toys.

Just because you have no habit, though, does not mean you are protected from the perils faced by those dealers with a habit. With the exception of shitting your own bed, all those perils still exist, and more.

Add to this the fact that the drug business is, arguably, the most paranoid business in the world because it involves selling an illegal product to people who are desperate for it. With its value and demand, selling dope is also one of the most profitable businesses in the world.

I have a few questions for you. Look around you at everybody you know who happens to know that you deal drugs, who among them do you trust with your life or your freedom? You need to be able to trust all of them, which we both you know you do not and cannot, and don't forget, the more successful you become the greater the reward for getting you busted.

Do you think your buddies will never talk? Are you that stupid; do you watch television, read the newspapers, or are you too busy poisoning people to bother doing so?

The individual who started a well-known gang in the lower mainland of British Columbia testified against his gangsta buddies in the murder of six people in Surrey, B.C. Every major biker gang in Canada and the USA has had full patch members turn against them, and even La Cosa Nostra is rife with informants, but you think you are special. You think nobody will rat you?

Do you remember when they used to bring dope into the country 200, 300, or even 500 kilos at the time? Well, those days are basically gone because somebody almost always ratted the load and those were big loses to incur.

How many people would you let know that you had 200 kilos coming in? Obviously, very few. So, who do you think tipped the cops about those loads? Do you think it might have been a "higher up" guy or a close friend? Of course, it was; they were the only ones who knew.

Now they bring it in 50, 80 or 100 kilos at a time to avoid the big loses. The problem with this new strategy of downsizing the loads is that doing so requires more transactions to import the same amount of dope, and the greater the number of transactions, the greater the risk of getting caught.

If you successfully dodge the "buddy fucked me up trap" for awhile, if you are dealing and not using, what do you do with the money? If you are dealing and using, it is obvious where the money goes, into your rig or into your pipe.

You can't just start throwing your money in the bank; there will be too many questions. You can't start flashing, buying fancy cars, draping yourself in jewelry, clothing yourself in expensive threads, and living in a high-end condo. This will draw attention to you and all law enforcement need do is look at what you own, versus what you legitimately earn, and you are done again.

Once you are targeted, law enforcement will study your organization looking for the weak link, and looking for the person who is unhappy with you or the person who has a dope habit. They will find that person and use that person to bring you down.

Maybe it will be a jilted lover, or an employee, or an acquaintance who believes he was treated unfairly, or dissed by you. Maybe it will be one of your friends who might be feeling too much heat and wants to deflect it to you. The possibilities are endless.

When they do arrest and convict you, they will take all your cars, all your jewelry, all your clothes, all your fancy electronics, and all your real estate. Therefore, you worked hard to build up everything you have with no chance to enjoy it. It gets worse, though.

With you in custody or jail, the informant who turned you in will be free to turn in others and to put it on you as being the rat because you are in jail, and therefore, have incentive to rat and because he/she has the freedom of movement and the freedom to talk to anybody in your little crime family without you knowing, a freedom you do not enjoy.

Every little break you might get because of your high-priced attorney will be used against you by the informer, as he/she uses those breaks you got as proof that you are ratting now to buy favors and to get your sentence reduced.

When you eventually come out of jail, if you actually make it out alive, which you probably will, you will come out with nothing. Everything you gained by destroying families will have been taken by the Office of Forfeiture, and you will have a hard time finding a decent job because you have a criminal record.

Accordingly, you will go right back into slinging dope, but this time without your old buddies who, if they are not already in jail, probably want little to do with you because you are radioactive. Hell, they might even be looking to leave you dead or beaten up in an alley somewhere.

Of course, none of this takes into account the fact that the more successful you become, the more people with whom you will have to deal, and the more successful you become, the more you will be a target of gangs because you are cutting their grass.

You are going down at some point and nobody you know will give a damn because the type of people you hang with don't like you for your character because you have none, and they only really cared about the money you produced for them, or the money you spent on them trying to buy their friendship and respect.

They have no friendship or respect to sell you and none to give you because they are as lost in this world as you are, chasing dreams built on their customers chasing dragons. Dope is the devil without a very good disguise and you guys supply it to the world out of greed and without remorse.

In the end, which will come sooner than you imagine, all you will have are memories and misery, memories of how you used to be a baller, and misery built on the realization that you destroyed your life.

Remember, among others, they got Chapo Guzman, Pablo Escobar, Hector Beltran Leyva. In fact, the Mexican government, which is arguably less effective than American or Canadian authorities, says it has captured or killed more than eighty of Mexico's one hundred and twenty-two most wanted drug lords. Authorities say most have been caught alive.

If authorities got them, they will get you too. Most of those narco kings instilled more fear in people than you could ever hope to, lived in fortresses, controlled armies larger than many countries have, and had more money with which to hide than you could imagine.

If you want to dance to the music, then you will eventually have to pay the fiddler, and when your day eating mess with two hundred guys and working out in an exercise yard surrounded by barbed wire finally does come, which it will, if you have kids, those kids will be much older when you get out, and perhaps, be calling somebody else, "Dad." And that is probably rightfully so because you abdicated your rights to be called "dad" when you destroyed their lives by destroying your life.

Wherever your kid goes to school, he/she will be branded and teased for being the son/daughter of that "asshole drug dealer," and the label will follow him/her into job searches, etc., until he/she might finally be able to prevail over your legacy by showing enough ethics to overcome the label you put on him/her. (You'll just have to hope that the kid didn't learn ethics from you.)

To have that strength of mind and that strength of character to avoid your teachings, your kids would need to have learned the right things from somewhere else, as they sure could not have learned them from you, because if you were around for a few years when you weren't in jail, all your kids learned is that you were a dope-slinging criminal with criminal friends. That's the role model you became.

If your woman has half a brain, she will probably have moved on. What happened to your dreams of happy riches? How many generations will it be before a real man finally arises from the ashes of your family tree and puts the family you destroyed on the correct path in life?

So, you want to get rich being a nonuser-dealer, huh? Then you deserve everything bad that happens to you. May you rot in hell, and may a band of demons drag you for eternity by a white powdered chain, through piles of used syringes, and may every one of those syringes poke you and infect you with the pain of each life you helped to destroy. You are scum.

<u>User-dealers who used to be nonuser-dealer</u>

Shakespeare's Hamlet spoke of being "hoist by your own petard"; nowadays, it's called "karma." It's an often seen sight in the hood.

You will see many a nonuser-dealer ballin' (rolling large) his/her way past the countless lives he/she destroys, thinking himself/herself important. Then, a year later you might see that same individual after having tried and gotten addicted to that which he/she sells, skidded out and sketched out, with raw, red skin stretching over his/her boils, fifty pounds lighter and begging for a point of down, or for your spare change, or even for a cigarette.

The physical condition of these individuals touches the heart until one remembers how they got where they are and realizes that it is justice. When I see people in this condition and know them not to have previously been nonuser-dealers, I gladly offer a smoke or a toonie, hoping that my small courtesy might lighten their load a little, at least for a few minutes. Far more often than I could afford, I've been known to find $20 for them to get unsick.

On the contrary though, when I recognize them as previously having been a nonuser-dealer, I give them nothing, not even the kill (last few drags) from my cigarette. Let them live the life that they sold to others for their own greed.

<u>Dealers who sell to kids</u>

You rank with those like the scum in Chapter 1 who was sexually defiling the fifteen-year-old girl. Just as with the sexual molestation of a child, you are stealing children's innocence and replacing it with something that will haunt those children for the rest of their lives. When it comes to you, I recall a tee-shirt that I used to see some military wearing when they were off duty. It read, "Shoot first, let God sort it out later."

While I am not advocating such a vigilante approach, I certainly understand the sentiment when applied to you, whether you are a user or not. Just to be absolutely clear, I know many dealers who feel exactly as I feel – yes, some dealers have teenage kids – and I will go to them trying to find out who you are.

I make you this promise, if I ever get even the tiniest hint that you are dealing to our kids, whether alcohol, pills, weed, or whatever, I will also talk to every street and gang contact that I have, and I have more than you probably believe; I'll get your complete name and then give it to every cop I know.

I will then publicize your name in every manner of which I can think, and I can think of many, as I attempt to build for you the same future you are building for our youth.

CHAPTER 29

GANG ACTIVITY

A former gang member friend of mine broke it down this way: **"All my friends are being prosecuted, are in jail, or are dead. I got out of the gang lifestyle because I realized that if you want to be a drug dealing gangster, you have no future and end up with nothing because you'll either get caught or get shot."**

Did you forget already? There is no significant gang activity here because the police keep the gangs out and keep you safe. Do you get it yet?

It falls on the police and on you people on the street to maintain it that way. The police cannot do it alone and the street cannot do it alone. In fact, if the street goes about protecting itself from gangs with the same cunning with which it goes about peddling its poison, we are all doomed; so, I'm going to give you a quick gang primer.

You will recognize any potential gang incursion(s) when somebody tells you that you must buy from this person or that person or when somebody tells you that you are not allowed to sell here or sell there, or when somebody tells you to whom you may sell or from whom you may buy.

Gangs need this type of control to take over a territory, town, or even a street corner. Without that control, you are in control of what you do, instead of them, and they will not make enough money to maintain their large inventories or support their lavish lifestyles.

Please understand that I am not talking about the mafia type of organized crime here, but about the dope slinging gangs, with loose organization, the members of which do drive by shootings and murder innocents who just happened to be in the wrong place at the wrong time.

Gang are like cock roaches; once they get any kind of a foothold, they will multiply and before you know it, your town/city will be infested. If you want to keep your town/city gang free and maintain any control, you need to alert the police if you see anything that you believe resembles gang activity in town. I can guarantee you that if any gangs get a foothold your way of life will change for the worse.

I am not suggesting that you sell or use dope; but, if you do, whether you are a user-dealer or just a user, there are other things you can do. Chief among them, do not buy your dope from anybody who is not an addict. Do not buy from people whom you do not know; and if possible, do not buy from any dealers unless you know from whom they buy.

Also, be wary of anybody who wants to front you a lot of dope, offers you prices below the market, seems to have kilos, tells you they can protect your territory, or just seems powerful. These are all warning signs of gang connections, and even if not connected today, you need to avoid knowingly enriching the pockets of major players because they will be the primary, initial, takeover targets when the gangs do attempt to invade. Thus, they will be connected in the near future.

Gangs love to suck you in and get control of you by fronting you, or offering you great prices, or having really pure dope, or offering you protected territories. After a short time, the fronting stops, the great prices go up considerably, the pure dope is cut so deep that you can't really get high off of it, and the protected territories come with demands that you sell a certain amount, or else. If you have already been sucked in, or do get sucked in, call the cops when you figure it out or after the cheap dope ends.

I realize that giving you what they promise you early on is very appealing if you are slinging, but again, it's a trap. Don't take the bait because I guarantee you that when things go bad, and they will go bad, you will be one thrown under the bus. And, throwing you under the bus could mean you taking the fall for whatever crime they need you to cop to, or you ending up dead because you know too much about their operation, or you just take a severe beating.

I have a friend in an extremely well known and prolific gang who calls me from prison. He calls me because his fellow gang buddies won't take his calls anymore. They never visited him and only sent him a few dollars exactly twice and then abandoned him. You are replaceable, and therefore, expendable just as he was. There is always another fool who sees only the riches or street respect (fear) and is willing to buy into the gang lifestyle bullshit.

That is the family he adopted looking for acceptance, looking for love, and looking for security. Cold hearted, greedy bastards don't have any of the above to give.

To make matters worse, when you do get busted, which you will, you will owe the gang for all the dope that was taken during the bust, including a possible "street tax" or "stupid tax" (a penalty imposed on you by the gang because they can get away with it due to intimidation). You'll be fucked and might be expected to commit some heavy duty crimes to cover your debt, if indeed, you are actually given that opportunity instead of being called a bitch and tossed into some ditch.

When you are dealing with gangs, the dope business is no longer just a game of cat and mouse between you and the cops. Gangs are about two things, money and control through brutality. They don't care about you, about your woman, or about your family. In fact, they will threaten your woman and your family to increase their control if you open the door even a crack to allow them into your life.

You ladies who work the street are a valuable line of defense because you will be among the first people whom the gangs will attempt to control by demanding that you buy dope from a particular person. You are also the most vulnerable because you willingly walk up to and climb into cars when you have no idea who the driver might be.

CALL THE POLICE AS SOON AS THE FIRST DEMAND IS PUT ON YOU. The police will protect your anonymity and initiate the process of identifying your intimidator.

All of you need to be vigilant and ruthless in making the police aware of what is happening with any possible gang activity. It is the only way to protect yourself.

This does not mean that the cops can protect you 24/7 because they cannot protect you from your lifestyle, but they will make you as safe as they possibly can, given the risk factors that you create for yourself.

Any information will help the cops protect you: a phone number, a street name, a description of a guy or of a car, and if you are vigilant, a license plate number. When you see a friend or other working girl climb into a car, make a mental note of any information you observe. You never know when it might become important information with which to protect you.

The bottom line here is that if you don't do these things, you are putting yourself in more danger because you are inviting gangs and violent bullies to control your life. Again, you can do all this without a single soul knowing.

Do you want to see the reality if you don't or won't do these things to protect yourself, your bros, your girl, your hood, and your family from gangs? Let me give you a couple of interesting quotes from www.gangstersout.com and www.gangstersout.blog.ca.

Now let's pause and look at Janice Shore's brutal murder. She was brutally beaten and raped in public on a Sunday morning and left where everyone would see her to send a message. The Surrey Leader reported that one source told them she was killed for a drug debt. Those that knew her said it couldn't have been a large debt because she was a user not a dealer. No doubt that is who they target to use as examples.

"Janice was a nice person. She was quiet, polite, and friendly. She also struggled with a mental illness. What kind of predator gives a quiet homeless woman with a mental illness free drugs then beats the life out of her for payment. Giving the homeless and the

mentally ill free drugs then beating them and torturing them for payment is predatory. It is total low life. That is as low as you can go.

They scratched out one of Janice's eyes. They caved in the side of her head and her jaw. There was absolutely no need for that kind of brutality. These are not the people we should be letting sell drugs in public, let alone pay them for heroin at the unsafe injection site. When we let them sell drugs in public, we endorse their brutal violence and their exploitation of the poor, homeless, and the mentally ill.

We don't need to harass the addicts. We need to harass the predatory drug dealers that profit from that kind of violent exploitation. We need to arrest the drug dealers not the drug addicts...."

How about this one? *"A new term known as working off minutes has begun in northern Alberta. It means enduring 1 minute of torture for every $100 owed. People who wear a Hells Angels support shirt now aren't just saying support your local crack dealer. Now they are saying they support torture, murder, decapitation, and dismemberment. They are saying they are deranged"*

Or how about this one? *"Sitting in the witness box, the slender woman, now 33, explained how Anderson and his then-girlfriend Melissa Senko had lured her to a hotel room, and tried to force her to agree to a scheme that would allow them to collect on a debt owed to the unnamed third party.*

They told her they wanted her to do "jobs" to pay back the alleged loss, and also offer up a weekly sum they'd use to keep a lawyer on retainer, should they be caught for any misdeeds.

To ensure the victim's compliance, Senko spent hours torturing and degrading her while Anderson stayed nearby offering his support.

"He didn't have the guts to defend me," said the victim.

And, she explained, she could have used the help. By night's end, Senko subjected her to degrading full-body searches, hateful comments, knife-wounds to her face and arm that needed medical intervention, as well as numerous burns to her legs and back.

When the night started, however, Anderson indicated to the victim she could avoid what was to come.

"He said, 'just tell the truth, tell the truth and it will be easier for you,'" she recalled.

"Then (Senko) punched me in the face. I said I wasn't guilty, 'please let me go' and I was crying."

It seemed, from her perspective, however, that Senko was enjoying the work at hand.

"She said, 'I'm not finished yet, I need to show you what I'm made of'," she said.

"She was becoming adrenalized with the fear she was putting in me."

That's when she tried to walk out of the hotel room, but Anderson intervened pushing her back to the hotel bed.

"I panicked and I went for the house phone," she said. "I tried to dial out, then she grabbed the handset, hit me in the head (with it) and almost knocked me out — I saw stars."

Other hits followed, as the night unfolded and the sight of the victim's blood prompted an unusual response from her captors.

"When she got a good shot in, they'd high five," she said.

They also took photos and video.

"(Senko) said there wasn't enough blood, and she needed to get a few more shots in to make the pictures look good," she said.

It was Anderson who was taking the pictures and shooting video footage.

As the night progressed, a second attempt at escape offered the window to freedom.

At the end of another struggle with Senko, the victim was knocked to the bed and landed near her cell phone, which had earlier been taken away.

She grabbed the phone and slipped it into her bra, under her armpit and shortly thereafter Anderson and Senko started "taking hoots" from their crack-pipe.

The pipe, which had a long hose and a glass stem didn't distract them for long, however.

Senko ended up using it burn the victim.

"I have a lot of burn (scars) on my back and legs," she said.

Then the knife came out, and the struggle left the victim with several gashes.

"I can remember the look on her face—she was so excited and so pumped up," she said. "She was like a kid at Christmas."

The night's damage was bloody, and eventually the victim was allowed to go to the bathroom. First Anderson helped clean her wounds, then she was permitted a small window of time to use the facilities.

That's when she uncovered the phone she'd stashed, and kept hidden, despite the duos attempt to find it.

She hid it under a towel on her lap and dialed [sic] 911, and when the call was answered she whispered the hotel's name and room number, twice.

A short time later the police arrived and the victim was able to tell them what happened through a torrent of tears.

Although Senko, who was sentenced to three years, was the main aggressor, Anderson played a significant role in the crime. He also has a lengthy criminal history of violence."

How about one more? September 24th the Calgary Sun reported that police found 10 kilos of crystal meth and 260 grams of crack cocaine in one vehicle and found even more crystal meth in a second vehicle along with powder cocaine and more crack.

Jason Quinn Antonio, 38, of Calgary was charged with two counts of possession for the purpose of trafficking and one count of possession of proceeds of crime. Jose Rodolfo Cruz Rivera, 59, of Calgary was been charged with one count of trafficking a controlled substance.

Now the Calgary sun is reporting that Jason Quinn Antonio was shot dead behind his home 10:00 AM yesterday morning. Sadly, he likely wasn't shot because he was a crystal meth dealer. He was more likely shot so he wouldn't rat out the ones he worked for and because he was now liable for the debt the seizure incurred.

Do you understand what is at stake now? Is that the way you want to live? This is what you invite when you allow gangs and bullies to go unchallenged because you want to believe in some moronic, non-existent street code. You are sowing the seeds of your own destruction. You NEED to prevent this from happening where you live.

You also need to realize though that police cannot overlook you selling or committing other crimes just because you have helped with the gangs. The benefit you will get for your help is the knowledge that nobody is, or will be, controlling you or your significant other. That should be all the benefit you should require because if any gang gets a foothold, it will own your ass. Just look at the above-related stories and understand what is coming if you continue to believe in some non-existent street code.

So, yet again, when the cops roll by, give them a wave or nod of thanks for protecting you, your woman, your children, and your family. They may play for a different team than you, but you share a common enemy, namely gangs. Again, you need to remember that the enemy of your enemy is your friend and the cops are the enemy of your enemy, the gangs.

You and the cops can be on opposing teams and still show each other mutual respect. Therefore, as it is inevitable that you get arrested, give the cops the respect of keeping your pie hole shut, and instead, if you still intend to follow your life of crime, which is not something I am advocating, resolve to be smarter in the future, because the cops obviously outsmarted you this time, as they always eventually will.

As for you gang bangers, you have your street code, but it's a code of disgrace, not a code of honor. And when you go to jail, you'll be out of sight and out of mind; you will be forgotten; all that "bro" shit won't exist any more. You'll just be considered another loser doing your time like my gang-banger friend in prison.

CHAPTER 30

CHILD ABUSE

Carolyn Ainscough: "The abuser's desire to abuse is not created by the child – it is there before the child appears."

Robert Fulghum: "Don't worry that children never listen to you; worry that they are always watching you."

I apologize to you, my reader, for my lack of courage and resolve in only possessing the emotional strength to deal with child abuse very briefly in these few short paragraphs, and then, only with the sexual abuse aspect thereof because my anger is so dissipated on the sexual abuse of children aspect that I would be unable adequately to communicate the sorrow and rage I feel at all aspects of this sickness that infects generations of our society.

Although my thoughts here are principally fueled when thinking of girls, as opposed to boys, I do have sympathy for the boys who are sexually abused, but maybe because I am a man and believe men should have a greater capacity to recover emotionally (again my ignorance I am certain), I cannot feel the same rage when thinking of boys without, at least, considering the age at which the abuse occurred/started.

That is my shortcoming and a personal shortcoming I am working to improve. Nevertheless, my bias toward believing that males must be men cannot avoid being incorporated into the manner in which I think and express myself in many areas of this book, including this chapter.

All victims of abuse, as well as those who are aware of any child who is being abused, please read the quote that prefaces this chapter. Now read it again; reread it; memorize it if you have to, and do whatever it takes to bring it into your core beliefs and into your soul.

Once it is part of you, shout it and whisper it to every victim of sexual abuse whom you might encounter, and if you are a victim, know in your heart that what occurred was never your fault, never could have been your fault and never can be made to be your fault unless you wrongly make it so.

Make this knowledge a mantra if that is what it takes, or perhaps accept those words as a divine gift from God. Look at other children who you now see and observe their innocence; know that their innocence is fragile and beautiful and understand that it needs protection.

Please realize that if you were a victim, you used to feel that innocence. It was once yours and it still is yours, you did not give it away, but instead, some sick bastard just buried it deep inside you.

It remains there, waiting for you to dig into your heart and mind with the shovel of your tears and pain, waiting for you to unearth it again and in so doing, to recover your self respect and your life.

You have three lives. You are who you used to be, who you are now, and who you can be. You cannot change the first life. It is a burden put upon you by the sick mind of a deviate abuser.

You can only begin to change the second life (who you are) by looking at the third life (who you can be) and having the courage to put the first life behind you by properly assigning the blame for the abuse you suffered during childhood. It is literally a shame that it occurred, but it is not your shame; no, the shame belongs to your abuser. Set aside the false guilt and begin building your third life today.

Look at with whom you associate and look at your daily habits, then analyze whether or not they take you to your third life or whether or not they keep you trapped in limbo between your first life and your second life. When you find the strength to choose the third life (who you can be), rather than continue being a victim, you will have the tools to be a victor.

Seize that quote from the beginning of this chapter and start your journey to your dreams. Start putting your nightmares behind you and begin the change to who you can be.

I believe in you and you will find others who also believe in you. Seek those people; you will recognize them by their honesty, by their compassion and by their lack of judgmental statements against you because of what was done to you. Seek them out and begin to believe in yourself. May God bless you on your journey and may the winds of change inspire you with the hope you deserve.

CHAPTER 31

TO ABUSED WOMEN

Your ass is not your boyfriend's dope supplier and if he loved you or had any respect for you he would not accept your dope or your money and would not abuse you in any way whatsoever. Get rid of the loser, and if you believe you need a man to feel complete, then find a man, but women using and abusing scum are not men; they are a disease, an infection and an abomination.

Eric Hoffer: "You can never get enough of what you don't need to make you happy."

With the release of this book, I am announcing the launch of a new website, soon to be started by a good friend of mine, www.womenabusersarescum.com. It is my hope that proceeds from the sale of this book will help him support his website.

The purpose of this website is to give women a forum in which to anonymously post information about male abusers. In an ideal world, the women will post as much information as they can about these abusers, such as the city in which they reside (anywhere in North America), the area of the city they frequent, their age or DOB, their name, how often they beat you or other women, their occupation, even a photograph of the abuser if you have such, and whether or not they have young children.

If you want, you can post a description of exactly what the abusive scum did to you (possibly losing anonymity in so doing). Such pictures will drive home the danger posed by the abuser to an even greater degree.

If you know a woman-abusing scum, by all means anonymously post the information. You do not have to be the victim to post. The more people who post about what happened to a friend, the less the possibility that the abuser can think that he may have been pinpointed by any particular tipster.

I want to help grow my friend's site to the point that any woman can look up a potential male (not to be mistaken with a "man," because women-abusing males are nothing more than bitch boys) and determine whether or not she wants to take the risk of being with that male.

If you are abused, you owe it to yourself and to other women to warn them of a scumbag abuser. It is time to put an end to these cretins who get their rocks off abusing women.

Again, you may post anonymously or put your name there. This is an absolutely free service; it will not cost you even one cent. The site will be funded entirely through donations and possibly advertising. Additionally, the site will provide contact information about governmental resources to which women can turn for help.

If you are an individual who shares my disdain for women abusers and would like to offer these abused women your assistance, my friend will be compiling a list of "real men" and "courageous ladies" who would be willing to assist these abuse victims to court to testify, to the hospital for treatment, and to a counselor for help. To protect the victims, if you do volunteer, there will be a vetting process to assure that you are genuine.

Finally, www.womenabusersarescum.com will also feature a petition to be presented to the government and to the courts, pleading with each of those entities dramatically to lengthen the sentences abusers must endure, especially for repeat offenders. There will be a mechanism online whereby you can add your name to this petition. It is critical that you do so. Those names added to the petition will not be published, but my friend cannot guarantee what the government might do with them.

These abusive scumbags should have no place to hide and should be severely punished for their repulsive behaviors. All of you, as individuals, can expose abuse and protect women in our society. You can help to stamp out these vermin who abuse women.

If you are an abused woman living amongst those who preach "street code," those in the hood would like you to believe that anytime you call the cops you are a rat. Your abuser needs you to worry about being labeled a rat because if you are afraid that calling the cops to protect yourself makes you a rat, your abuser can continue to make you a victim; he can control you because you are presented with Hobson's choice. He wants to give you the choice of thinking that you can either get your ass kicked for being a rat or that you have to tolerate him kicking your ass. It's a lie.

The truth is that you do not need the street's permission or approval to call the police. Not only is it your right to call the police anytime you feel violated, it is also your obligation to do so to protect others who might follow you in a relationship with the monster who abuses you.

You might think that you will be all right if you don't piss him off, but with abusive males, they will always find a reason to beat you anyhow, even if you are perfect, because they can't allow you to believe you are right, or good, or perfect because if you develop any sense of self-respect, you won't put up with their abuse any longer.

Of course, you don't want the street to label you a rat because you want acceptance. Just remember the cost of that acceptance. You have to allow your boyfriend/significant other to steal from you or you have to go to jail for committing crimes to protect him or you have to die at his hands, or maybe all three, in the order presented, of course.

Additionally, the more people who call the police, the less will be the stigma in doing so, eventually making calling the police the accepted and expected norm.

If you are not in anyway connected to "the street" and just don't want your friends and neighbors to know that you are abused, either because you are ashamed or because you are afraid, stop fooling yourself. Your friends probably already know and don't want to embarrass you. If you are scared now, you will be terrified later because the abuse will only get worse and will never end until you get the help you need to end it.

You say that you don't want to call the police because you love the guy. I say that's a crock of crap; you don't love the guy; you might love being abused by the guy because he may have convinced you that you deserve the abuse, or you may love the high that comes from your fear or you might think that abuse is love because that is the lesson that you took from your childhood.

Abuse is not love, never has been and never will be. Post on www.womenabusersarescum.com, CALL THE COPS, and call your local women's support group.

Not only do you not love the guy, the guy does not love you. He loves abusing you; he loves seeing you scared because it makes his smarmy ass feel powerful; he loves controlling you because the rest of his life is so out of control, and if you are from the street, he loves the dope or the money you bring him and he loves the free sex, but he doesn't love you. He never really did and he never will.

Think about this, if you believe that he loves you, you had better pray to God that he doesn't also love your kid(s) as much as he says he loves you. Most of these guys can talk a polar bear out of a seal pup when it comes to convincing you how much they love you, how worthless you are and how sorry they are that they hit you; don't believe their bullshit.

If he loved you, he wouldn't hit you. He is not even capable of love, thinking abuse is love, just as you might think it is. Post on www.womenabusersarescum.com, CALL THE COPS, and call your local women's support group; then get as far away from your victimizer as quickly as you can.

Take your life back. Just because you lack self-respect due to how you make a living, or because you do dope or for whatever reason you might have fabricated in your mind doesn't mean that you have to tolerate his abuse and the disrespect it heaps on you.

You might not be able totally to regain your self-respect until you make some other changes in your life, but you can start. You can grab it back a little bit at a time. It all begins with you not accepting abuse from anyone.

Why should you be the one who is afraid? Your abuser should be the one who is afraid, and he will be if he knows that you or any woman who witnesses his abuse will call the cops. Put him in fear.

The problem is that these abusive, male vermin like to commit their vile acts in private, instinctively knowing that they are wrong, but not giving a damn. You can still get help though by calling police and showing police the results of his abuse.

Don't lie to yourself either and say you are staying for the dope; that's bullshit and you know it. If you want to run that spin at me, I have a question for you. If some guy picked you up on the stroll and offered to give you $80 if he could beat the shit out of you, would you accept the deal? Stop with the idiotic excuses. Post on www.womenabusersarescum.com, CALL THE COPS, and call your local women's support group.

Perhaps you were attracted to this guy because you initially found him exciting. If that is the case, then you need to stay away from guys whom you find exciting; that excitement is your warning bell; it is simply the smell of a new car before you've driven it for a week or have to call the mechanic for the first time; it is your subconscious telling you that this guy is a woman beater. You need to look for a man whom you find interesting or even boring, not exciting.

You need to understand that what you have been through and what you are now experiencing is as good as it will ever be with your exciting guy. It only gets worse from here.

Women abusers always escalate their behaviors. They just keep beating you and the beatings become more and more severe as they try to exercise more and more control. If you are an abused woman, post on www.womenabusersarescum.com, CALL THE COPS and your local women's support group before the one you say you love kills you.

Stop lying to yourself. The most insidious and damaging of all lies we tell are the lies that we tell ourselves. Post on www.womenabusersarescum.com, CALL THE COPS, and call your local women's support group. Any cell phone with a SIM card, with time or not, can call 911. DO IT!!!!

In closing this chapter I need to deal with one thing that really rankles me which is boyfriends who brand their women. Don't accept the tattoo ladies.

If he was a real man and if truly loved you, he would get a steady job, provide a stable home for you and ask that you accept his ring on your finger instead of putting his name on your ass. Where I grew up, men branded their cattle, not their women.

END OF CHAPTER QUESTIONS

16. Do you think child abuse leads the child to drug addiction?
17. Do you think that women get addicted to being abused?

Post your answers on www.breakingthecode.ca.

CHAPTER 32

TO ABUSIVE MALES

www.womenabusersarescum.com

Whenever somebody tells me that some woman-abusing scum is in jail, I always ask, "What is he in for, besides not nearly enough time?"

If you claim abuse as your excuse for abusing, you should know that the toxic element in your relationship(s) is you; you need to work on you and control you and leave her the hell alone.

My friend's new web site will "out" every last one of you assholes. It will make you wear what you do because it will unrelentingly tie your actions to your name for all to see, hopefully forever.

Sam Houston: "Remember that whatever may be said by a lady or her friends, it is not part of a gallant or generous man to take up arms against a woman."

Jonathan Swift: "I never wonder to see men wicked, but I often wonder to see them not ashamed."

If you are a woman beater or an emotional or a verbal abuser of women, you are pond scum. To you males who abuse women, I quote Mark Twain, who said, "I didn't attend the funeral, but I sent a nice letter saying I approved of it."

Having a few parts hanging between your legs does not make you a man; it simply means that you are a male of the species, and there is a big difference between the two.

Whether you are a man will not be determined by the length of your wanker, the breadth of your shoulders or the size of your biceps; it will be determined by your actions and what those actions reveal about your character.

Allow me to ask you a few questions. Do you really think that she loves you, or do you think that she is just afraid not to pretend to you and to herself, that she loves you? Some children, when first getting potty trained, are afraid to flush their poop down the toilet; do you think those children really love their poop?

Does beating a woman make you feel like a man? Does it make you feel powerful that you have the strength to beat up a woman? Does her fear of you excite you?

What about telling her she is worthless and calling her vile names? Does that make you feel important? Does it make you feel successful? Does it make you feel better than her?

If she is so worthless, why do you want to be with her? I know, you are going to say that you are just trying to help her get her life straight because you love her so much. Bullshit!

Do you love her so much that you want to see her live in fear; do you think that is healthy for her?

Beating a woman is all about your rage, your lack of real self esteem and your inadequacies. You are a worthless piece of shit with your lies, your abuses, and your excuses. When the woman you abuse finally finds the courage to get away from you, she will look back on you as the asshole with whom she used to live.

As an abuser, you have no character, so you are not a man; you are a lousy excuse for a human being. A man has character and a man controls his anger.

In the real world and in my world, you are not a man if you hit a woman; in the real world and in my world, you are not a man if you sit on your ass and allow a woman to risk her freedom or risk anything else to support you, and if you have a habit, allow her to support your habit.

In the real world and in my world, unless and until you consistently get off your ass and do what has to be done to take care of your woman and yourself and unless and until you do what has to be done to seek to ensure that you will be able to be there in the future to ensure her well being, you are a loser and a Neanderthal.

If your reaction to this is that you want to kick my ass, then that reaction just proves my point. Would it make you proud to lay a beating on the 68-year-old man who has suffered through seven heart attacks; will that prove to yourself or anybody else that you are a man?

All it would prove is your ignorance, your cowardice to face the truths in your life, and your inability to actually be a man. Is your search for self-respect, power, and manhood so desperate that you have to abuse women and beat old men? You may as well eat bananas all day, grunt, and drag your knuckles when you walk.

The problem with this analogy is that I must now apologize to the first ape I see as my comparison with you to apes insults apes as even apes do not abuse the females of their species. What does that fact say about you?

My mother was an alcoholic and both she and my dad were dead by the time I was fourteen. From that point, my brother and sister and I were split apart by a cunningly vicious alcoholic woman and by the time I was in my mid-teens, I ended up living without my real family. By my late teens I was alone until I grew into manhood and created my own family. Oh, did I mention that before the start of all this I was an international kidnap victim?

I don't care about your "boo hoos" and I don't want to hear how tough your childhood was or how you learned your brutal ways from watching your father beat your mother or any other psychological crap about how your mother or father abused you.

Even if there is a grain of truth in your claims about your childhood, rather than subject others to the behaviors that you endured use those childhood experiences as a reason why you will never treat others as you were treated. In other words, get over it; get on with life and go find some manhood. You are just making excuses to give yourself permission to continue your contemptible behaviors.

Men have reasons why they used to do certain things and losers have excuses why they continue to do those things. Nobody gives a damn about your excuses. Grow some testicles.

If I ever witness you abusing a woman, I will call the police. I will testify against you, and I will do everything in my power to convince your victim also to testify against you, including trying to get her to a safe place where you cannot reach out and touch her, a place where professional counselors will work with her and plead with her to testify against you. Then, I will petition the judge to give you a maximum sentence.

If you don't believe I will turn you in, remember Prince, remember Lemay, and remember Crazy. If you know anything at all about me, you know I am willing to die in order to keep this promise.

I hope every woman who reads this book understands that she will find support from the police; from the courts; and from several governmental, quasi-governmental, and charitable organizations. There are special shelters and programs that will seek to ensure your safety. If you are an abused woman, post on www.womenabusersarescum.com and CALL THE COPS and your local women's support group.

If you are a male reading this book who finds abuse of women as odious as do I, then I beg you, stand beside me and help rid our society of these pond scum. These abusers should not be welcome anywhere in the world.

In my candid opinion, the laws in British Columbia need to updated to the point wherein if any physical marks are present on the woman, that the man must be arrested and must be held for court. Without the enactment of such laws, these male scumbags will continue their reign of terror.

As I said earlier, whenever somebody tells me that one of you women abusing scum is in jail, I always ask, "What is he in for, besides not long enough?"

If you are an abuser, I pray that God starts creating a special place in hell for you the moment that you ever abuse a woman again, and I pray that a band of female demons escorts you to that place and beats on you there for eternity.

To you women abusers:

1. A man does not live off the proceeds of his woman's ass. That makes him a pimp, not a man.
2. A man does not hit his woman. That makes him a bitch, not a man.
3. A man does not call his woman vile names. That makes him an abuser, not a lover or a man.
4. A man does not put his woman down. That means the only way he can rise is to force his woman below him and that makes

him a loser, not a man.

5.   A man does not create babies that he cannot support. Making babies he cannot support makes him a sperm donor, not a father or a man.

A man puts himself between his woman and anything or anybody that threatens her self-respect, threatens her femininity, or could physically harm her. A man demonstrates to his woman that abuse, whether physical, emotional, or mental is NOT love. A man holds his woman's well being in his heart before he holds her body in his arms.

A man does not try to control his woman; a man recognizes that if his actions merit the love of his woman, that her love will be there for him, and that if it is not there for him, that his solution is another woman, not beating the one he has. A man stands beside his woman and earns her love and respect by giving her love and respect.

A man provides for his woman and ensures that he will be there in the future to continue to do so. That means a man doesn't do things which could put him in jail. He cannot support his woman from jail, and he cannot show his kids love from a jail cell.

As far as providing for your woman goes, spotting for her when she heads to the stroll is not providing for her or protecting her. As we used to say about lies when I was growing up, "That dog don't hunt".

Maybe you can convince her that is why you go out there with her, but she wants to believe you. I, on the other hand, am not so naïve. I know why you are really out there.

You are not going out there to protect her; you cannot get into the john's car with her and go on the date with her; you cannot follow his car on foot; you cannot stop the john from beating her when he gets her alone, so what protection do you offer? Even if you did record the john's plate number, wouldn't your non-existent code prevent you from calling the police?

You are out there, not to protect her, but to know when she scores a date so you can know when you might expect her back, so you can plan on when you can get your dope from her selling her ass. You are not a man; you are a pimp.

If she takes longer than you like, or than you expect or doesn't come back with enough dope or money to make you happy, then she is in a lot of trouble with you, maybe gets beaten or called a slut You are not out there to protect her; you are a worthless, slimy piece of shit.

How about when you go to jail? What is your woman supposed to do then, being that your excuse for spotting for her is that you think she needs "protection" on the street? With you in jail, does she not suddenly need another guy to spot for her; after all, you wouldn't want her out there without protection, would you?

With you in jail, do you expect her to wait six months for you and remain faithful to you, eschewing any help she might need, for any reason, from another guy? You would never down dick her to others if she found another guy, would you?

It is your dumb ass that went to jail, so you broke the bargain, not her. If you really love her, then you should pray that the next guy with whom she hooks up takes proper care of her and is smart enough to stay out of jail so he can continue to care for her. Or, are you just upset because somebody else is abusing and beating her instead of you?

You don't own a woman. She is not chattel. A woman is free to be with anybody she wants after you break up with her or desert her by not being there for her, and she is free to walk away from you whenever she wants whether or not you are in jail.

You say you love her; then don't you want what is best for her? Isn't it best for her that she is protected? If you think this is wrong, then what happened to your precious "protection" logic now? You don't want some other guy "protecting" her? Your supposed protection has again been exposed for what it really is: p-i-m-p-i-n-g.

Let's try another few questions. Do you want money for jail canteen while you are in? Do you expect her to send you that money or else be called vile names for not doing so, or take a beating after you are released? How do you expect her to get that money, selling her ass? If a woman sells her ass to support you, what does that make you; do you remember?

If you want to have a woman, then take responsibility for having a woman and make certain that there is money available to provide for her when you go away. If you can't do that, then don't expect the woman to wait for you, and don't abuse her when she does what she has to do to support herself. It's called "manning up."

You say you love your woman? Then get off your lazy ass, get a job, and prove it. Love is not just a word; love is a series of actions. Quit just talking the talk and start walking the walk. If you won't or can't do that, then don't call yourself a man.

I recall many years ago when my roommate hit me in the face because

I refused to give her money for drugs. I sat down on the couch and she hit me again. I then sat on my hands as she hit me five or six more times. It hurt, but I knew I wasn't in danger, so I did not respond with violence or even by restraining her. I allowed her to punch her anger away, and once that anger was gone and she realized what she had done, she started crying.

In the twelve years that followed that incident, she never hit me again. I strongly believe that her refusal to resort to violence thereafter is because she did not achieve her goal which was to have me hit her back, so she realized the futility of that type of approach.

Some of you may think I was nuts not to respond with a smack of my own, or at least to restrain her. I have no issue with a nonviolent restraint of a woman in a similar situation; but, the bottom line is, unless a woman is attacking you with a weapon, you do not hit her.

I was black and blue, but my manhood (not that manhood) was intact. Now I ask you, "Who got hurt the worst in that episode, her or me? If you think it was me, then I have just wasted quite a few pages talking to you.

If you want to claim manhood, then start doing those things that a man does. Just because you fail at one aspect for a period of time doesn't mean that you have to continue to fail at all aspects or any other aspect.

Step number one in claiming manhood is that YOU MUST NEVER ABUSE A WOMAN AGAIN, NEVER, N-E-V-E-R. You can stop it; you just don't want to.

END OF CHAPTER QUESTION

18. Do you think that women who allow themselves to be abused were abused in some fashion by their parent(s)?
19. Should the arrest of women abusers be automatic and require that any suspected abuser appear before a judge before he can be released?

Post your answers on www.breakingthecode.ca.

CHAPTER 33

MAKING BABIES

Khalil Gibran: "You are the bows from which your children as living arrows are sent forth."

Unknown Author: "Children are always the silent victims of drug abuse."

I am about to discuss a very touchy subject, and I will attempt to do so with as much sensitivity as possible. Before doing so though, I will first quote philosopher Eric Hoffer who said, "The weakness of a soul is proportionate to the number of truths that must be kept from it," and I will treat you herein as though no truths need be withheld.

As you read, if it is your desire to be angry and offended, I am certain that you can find an excuse to do so. If instead, you choose to read this with an open mind and to try to understand what is being said while imagining a child's face and heart, you will find no excuse for anger at me or to be offended my words.

If you already have a child and you are still involved with dope or are in an abusive relationship, then this is important for you too, so that you can understand what that child's future might look like. As long as you can convince yourself that you child is okay and will continue to be okay, you will have found your excuse to continue doing drugs and to continue your lifestyle.

Also, sadly, as long as you can convince yourself your life or your child's life will never improve and that you will always be powerless to improve it, you have found yourself another excuse. Drug use and abuse come with built in excuses and rationalizations.

The truth is that your child is not okay and will not be okay without you consistently in his/her life every day, without you being clean and sober, and without you in an abusive relationship. The other truth is that it is within your abilities to change that life if you start NOW.

You can lie to yourself all you want, but you know I am telling you the truth. I hope this truth will start you down the path to reality and sobriety.

If you do not already have a child, then please don't have one until you are completely done with both dope and abusers. You need to be in a position to love that child as much as you would like, as much as that child needs your love, and as much as you wanted to be loved when you were a child. Living with dope or abuse will not allow this to happen.

There will be a temptation to have a child because you want to give him/her the love you missed. If you or your significant other is involved with dope or you are an abuser or being abused, you cannot give that love no matter how much you feel it.

As was said earlier, love is not just a feeling; it is a series of actions. Dope and abuse are absolutely antithetical to raising a child with the love that a child needs and deserves. It is that simple, and you know it, so don't lie to yourself and in so doing create another unhappy soul on this planet.

Some of you might think about going ahead anyhow with the plan because your parents or the parents of your significant other can care for the child. Are these the same parents whom you blame for the fact that you turned to dope or turned to abuse or turned to being abused? If yes, what a stupid idea!

Even if the answer was "no," why would you think that your child would grow up happy and healthy with surrogate parents? A child needs his/her real parent(s) or that child will spend his/her life wondering why he/she was not worthy of being loved. Is that what you want for this person whom you intend to shower with love?

If no family members are in the offing to take care of your child, do you think that you can love that child every day while he/she is in a foster home? If a child would feel unlovable because he/she is staying with his/her other family members instead of with his/her parent(s), how do you think that child is going to feel living in a foster home?

Can you guarantee the quality of the foster home? Hell no! Do you want to gamble with the system knowing that your child loses no matter who the foster parent(s) might be and that it is only a question of how badly that child loses?

Will your child be born addicted to heroin? Stop it please. Don't create another life headed for the same misery in which you find yourself. Where is your brain? In fact, thinking about that child, where is your heart?

A child will not save you from your addiction(s) or stop any abuse that might exist in your life. A child will not change your life for the better unless you are abuse free and drug free. Only you can change your life and you cannot put it on your baby to do for you what you refuse to do for yourself. Don't be so damn selfish!

Don't fool yourself with that bullshit about quality time either. Neither you, nor anybody else, can say that next Friday at 3:00 p.m. will be quality time. Quality time is something that occurs spontaneously because of a quantity of time. Without quantity there will not be quality.

As I did in a previous chapter, please allow me to close with a discussion of tattoos, a discussion for both mothers and fathers. A tattoo of your kid's name doesn't make that child feel loved or prove that you love him or her.

If you want everybody, including your child, to know you love him or her, you need to put that child's name in your heart, not on your arm or leg.

Tattoos are just words or pictures and love is far more than that, even far more than just an emotion. Love is felt only by actions that demonstrate love.

Tattoo your kid's name in your heart and it will be there for eternity and you will never have to feel guilty about your life again.

A child can be a joy in your life, but only if you create joy in that child's life. If you are in an abusive relationship or doing dope, you cannot create that joy, so don't create that life until you have fixed your own life.

CHAPTER 34

CREATING A LEGACY

We should never let the past define us as long as we still have a future.

Lee Iacocoa: "No matter what you've done for yourself or for humanity, if you can't look back on having given love and attention to your own family, what have you really accomplished?"

Carl Jung: "Children are educated by what the grown-up is and not by his talk."

Marcus Tullius Cicero: "The life of the dead is placed in the memory of the living."

It is, perhaps tritely, although rightly, said that every individual who walks this earth leaves behind a footprint. The footprint becomes that individual's legacy when others look back on that individual's life and make judgments about it.

In general, the more good that an individual did, John F Kennedy for example, or the more bad that an individual did, Hitler for example, the longer their legacy survives. No matter the longevity though, it always survives long enough to influence and impact the children of that individual.

What footprint are you putting down on this earth? What will be your legacy?

Remember, you determine the footprint, but others, including your significant other and your kid(s), as well as possibly some from the mainstream of society, not necessarily from the street or from the drug community, will determine your legacy according to the footprint you left behind for them to see.

What does your footprint say about you? Does it say you are a purveyor of poisons? Does it say that you helped destroy families? Does it say that you beat and abused women? Will the most vivid memories of you be in police logs and the courts?

Will your children talk about how you were always there for them, or will they try to remember the few times you might have actually visited them? Will they think and talk about how much you loved their mother, or will they recall and talk about how you beat and otherwise abused their mother?

Will your children think back about the tricycle you brought them for Christmas or will they try to recall if you ever even spent even a single Christmas with them? Will they remember the times when you had to go on a business trip, or will they remember the times you were off to jail, yet again?

Will their memories of you be as a loving parent or will they just remember the judge's gavel pounding heavily down announcing you as an unfit parent? Will they wake up in the middle of the night excited about how loved they feel, or will they startle themselves alert from a nightmare of loneliness that you created for them?

It is your footprint, and it will be your legacy. What does it say about you? Will your children think of you with fondness or will they think of you high on drugs and in a hurry to get your next fix or your next hoot?

If they are in a foster home, does their foster parent or guardian get them excited that you might be coming for a visit, or anticipate any occasional visit with trepidation? Will you be missed, or will people not even notice your absence, or worse yet, will you be appreciated by your absence?

Will you be your child's excuse for him/her doing drugs because you did drugs, because you were not around due to jail or your addiction, or because your child was present when you were being abused or when you were doing the abusing? What footprint will you leave alongside that of your child? What impression will your life imprint in your child's heart or mind?

When your child grows into adulthood and you flash through his/her mind, will he/she quickly suppress that thought because it is too painful, or will the muscles surrounding his/her mouth relax and the corners curl upward into a smile? With every action you take, you are making those decisions for your child right now.

Did you ever hear the song The Cat's in the Cradle by Harry Chapin? There is a haunting refrain therein, "I'm gonna to be like you dad; you know I'm gonna to be like you…."

Do you get it? Children grow up to be like their parent(s); is your life the life you want for your child?

Where does the cycle of addiction, or abuse, or of being an absentee parent end? Does it end with you or do you pass it on to your kids who perhaps pass it on to your grandchildren, and so on and so on and….? If the chain continues on past you, who can you blame but yourself when you had the opportunity to change the future of your family for generations to come?

Do you take all of the foregoing as a guilt trip and use it an excuse to convince yourself that all is lost? It is only lost when you stop trying. Get off the dope; get off the abuse; get off the excuses.

Man up or woman up and stop the cycle now. You are creating your legacy. What will be your epitaph, will it be, "Abuser addicted to drugs" or will it be "Loving parent dedicated to his/her family"? What are you writing in the book of your legacy?

Now think about this, if you sling dope, the questions above are questions that you are helping to create for other parents every time you sell a point of heroin or hit of crystal meth or a twenty rock. You are destroying families.

If you are addicted yourself and slinging da shit, you are not just destroying your life and the lives of your family members, you are also destroying other families and other lives.

Of all the people in the world, logic should tell you that as an addict, you should understand more than any group of people the damage that drugs do. Where is your head; where is your heart? Are you that deep into your addiction?

Stop doing the drugs and stop selling the drugs; instead, help to make it difficult, if not impossible, for the next person who is curious about dope to find any. I know many of you and many of you know me.

I can tell you, from talking with those of you whom I know, that most of you wish you had never started down the path of drugs, and as often as not, think about getting clean – but thinking ain't doing.

Your footsteps are already there, but they lead nowhere, instead forming a circle that represents where your addiction has taken your life, and where addiction will always take you. You can change that path and you can also change the path down which your child's footsteps will lead. You can stop the circle of drugs and the circle of loneliness that your child feels.

Does it stop with you, or do you not have the guts? Will you daddy up or mommy up knowing that every moment you delay is another tear on your child's cheek, another rip in your child's heart and another ounce of anger in your child's soul, or will your kids read these words in the future and try to find the courage that you didn't have, the courage for them to stop being like you were?

If you change the direction that your footprints lead, you also change your legacy; it is your choice. Remember, your legacy will be your actions and your kids' actions, because your children will react to you and your life will be reflected in their lives.

CHAPTER 35

A WORD TO OUR YOUTH

If you're expecting a lecture, you're reading the wrong book. I don't believe in lectures; I believe in truths.

<u>Truth Number One</u>: **I am not you and I cannot possibly understand what you are going through.**

<u>Truth Number Two</u>: **I care!!!!**

<u>Truth Number Three</u>: **All drugs are gateway drugs. They are the gateway to your own personal hell.**

<u>Truth Number Four</u>: **All drugs physically alter your brain.**

<u>Truth Number Five</u>: **Your brain will not be fully developed until you are in your twenties and the younger you are when you start drugs, the greater the chance you will end up a hopeless addict.**

<u>Truth Number Six</u>: **This is the time you are training your brain. You can train it to be weak or you can train it to be strong.**

I give you truth because truth is your best friend and the most powerful tool that you can ever possess.

Allow me to start with a question, "When the people in this book first convinced themselves to try drugs, do you think any of them thought that they would end up being addicted, being homeless, being toothless, begging for handouts on the street, going to jail, or dying of an overdose?"

As I said, I cannot possibly understand the pressures in your life or what you are going through. I do know this: you will find yourself in this chapter because I know the five main reasons why people start drugs.

1. They are bored and looking for fun or excitement.
2. They see who they think are cool people doing drugs and they want to be cool, too.
3. They feel unaccepted and lonely.
4. Somebody has convinced them that they are worthless or stupid or ugly and will never amount to anything.
5. They suffered a trauma or are suffering a trauma that they are afraid to tell anybody about and they just want to escape thinking about it.

If you are bored, get a job, take up a sport, join a school club, find a hobby, read about drugs on the internet, or volunteer somewhere. I guarantee you that drugs are not the answer to your boredom. The boredom you feel is healthy; it is telling you that you are maturing and that your brain needs something stimulating to help you continue to grow.

If you want to be part of the cool set, look at the people in this book and ask yourself how cool your buddies who are doing drugs will be in a few years. My friend, I promise you that in a few years those people will be looking at you with envy, wishing they were as cool and as together as you.

If you want to do drugs to be accepted, look through this book and see the group to which you want acceptance and realize that each of them found an excuse to try drugs. You will be accepted in the very near future. You will be accepted by colleges, by employers, and you will be loved, appreciated, respected and accepted by people with whom you can actually enjoy life rather than by those who are looking to rob you for drugs and money. If people around you are doing drugs, get different friends. These are not your friends. They are your enemies. They are lost and you cannot help them. You don't have the skill set.

If somebody has convinced you that you are worthless or stupid or ugly and will never amount to anything, don't prove them right by turning to drugs. Instead, prove them wrong by doing something with your life. You are only stupid if you become like many of the people in this book.

As far as ugly goes, the only ugly things I have ever seen in my life are those people who turn to violence to hurt people and those people with a spirit that tries to hurt people with their words. Drugs will make you ugly because drugs lead you to both of these.

If you have suffered a trauma or are suffering a trauma that you are afraid to tell anybody about and just want to escape thinking about it, drugs are not the answer because you will be running from the frying pan into fire and taking the frying pan with you. You can never escape from yourself; you can only heal yourself, but you will need help. What happened to you, or is happening, might make you feel guilty or worthless or ashamed. But, the truth (and remember, I believe in truth) is that it is somebody else's worthlessness that caused these feelings in you; it is somebody else who should feel guilty, and it is not your shame, but somebody else's shame.

If you found yourself anywhere in this chapter, you need to reach out to somebody you trust. Talk to your parents, and if you can't talk to them or are afraid to talk to them, talk to a big brother or a big sister. If you don't have an older sibling, talk to a religious authority in your life or to a teacher who you trust not to betray you. If not a teacher, then you can find a cop and talk to him or her. Most cops care about you more than you can understand. If you trust your school counselor, talk to him or her.

The important thing here is that you talk to somebody about any of these concerns. Don't fight your feelings by yourself. You can even send me an email at hal@breakingthecode.ca and I will find somebody for you. Just don't allow yourself to get lost to the drug world, and remember, addiction, especially at your age, might be almost unavoidable through even a single drug experience.

The truth is that if you start down the path of drugs, you will probably die a lonely death after suffering more pain than you can imagine. Ninety-nine percent of the people out there would be honored to have the opportunity to help you with whatever is pushing you to want to try drugs; so don't turn to drugs, turn to one of those people instead. I beg you.

I will give you one final truth. As much as I would like to promise you happiness, I cannot because I don't know if you will give yourself permission to be truly happy, instead of just to be high. What I can promise you though is that drugs are not the answer because you are guaranteed misery if you use drugs.

You are in my prayers.

END OF CHAPTER QUESTIONS

20. Do you think that a child suffers if he/she does not have a real parent as a continually active participant in that child's life?
21. Do you know any families that could benefit by reading this book?

Post your answers on www.breakingthecode.ca.

CHAPTER 36

YOUR LOVED ONE
WANTS TO GET INTO RECOVERY

I'm really happy for you, truly I am. What's next? Back up, shut up and listen; that's what's next.

Just because your loved one wants to get the monkey off of his/her back at the moment doesn't mean that it won't still be out there. Don't feed the monkey with old behaviors.

Sadly, often times what lays between the recovering son or daughter success are the parents who, afraid of another failure by their loved one, would rather shame the loved one than take the necessary self-inventory and determine what is the best thing they can do now. That best thing is often to just "get the hell out of the way."

It is a very distressing thing to watch somebody who wants recovery reach out to a parent and see that parent react as he/she has always reacted, thereby driving their loved one away. Do not forget that unresolved emotional conflicts within the addict are probably what started him/her down the road to drugs in the first place, so don't repeat old behaviors.

Here is the situation in a nutshell. This child of yours has hurt you and disappointed you so many times in the past that you don't want to set yourself up to be heartbroken again; you are afraid to believe, but deep down you really want to believe because you long for the love or trust that was there when he or she was ten years old. Hello! Welcome to your loved one's head space. He or she is feeling the exact same thing, going through the same angst and has the same hopes.

It is time for you to take stock of your life, not his life or her life, but of your own life, your spouse's life and the environment you provided that assisted in leading your loved one down the path to drugs. I'm not saying that he or she necessarily turned to drugs as a direct result of your actions. I'm not outlawing that possibility either.

More than likely, you missed a clue somewhere or some behavior coming from your home that was somehow, perhaps innocently and/or ignorantly, at least contributory. If you cannot do an absolutely self-honest assessment of who you are and what your behaviors and the stresses from those behaviors may have said or done to your loved one, then you are more worried and protective of yourself than you are of your loved one, step away.

You and your loved one are each renewing a relationship that was painful to you both, trying to get past old hurts and old betrayals. Think of how you would each react to one another if those memories did not exist for either of you, if you had never met. Your job, as would your loved one's job, would be far easier.

Neither of you would want to rush into each other's arms, nor be willing to give trust that had not been earned. Neither of you would be trying to control the other's life, nor talking to the other of the hurts each had caused the other.

Each of you must now put the past behind you; each of you must look at this as a relationship that is fresh, and in so doing, each of you must do what you would do if you had never met before, meaning that each of you must refuse to bring your baggage to a stranger's home or put your burden on a stranger's heart. If the recovery is successful, the time might come for dealing with those hurts, but it will be years down the line.

Each of you will recognize that time when you have built an entirely new relationship and when that new relationship has bonded into a relationship of mutual trust. When that happens, the bad times will then be looked at as a period that occurred between the joys of childhood and the now new joys of this new relationship.

Now though, it is time for self-control and this is where your self-inventory enters the picture. If you created too many expectations, forget the expectations. You have no room for expectations now; you only have room for hope and for prayer.

If you were a yeller, talk softly now. If you were a controller, yield that control with words such as, "that is up to you honey." If you were a criticizer, stop criticizing; instead, learn to lightly encourage with words such as, "It's your recovery sweetie and as much as I would like to help, I think the best thing for you is to work with professionals and walk the road you need to walk. I've always loved you and always will and cannot wait until I have you back."

This is a psychologically fragile time for you and your loved one and your hopes will be so high for him/her that any controlling instincts you may have had will rise to top and probably overpower and try to direct the recovery that excites you so much. Remember, this is his/her recovery, not yours, and you must allow him/her to walk his/her chosen road without any interference from you. This will be difficult, but it is critical that you do so.

Instead, tell that loved one that as much as you hope his/her recovery is real this time that it is, indeed, his/her recovery and that you don't want to mess it up in any manner. Tell him/her that you will try to be there when he/she reaches out to you, but that you will not be volunteering or offering advice as your doing so might be misinterpreted as interfering (Hell, it might actually be your instinct to interfere.) and that you do not want to get in the way of what he/she needs/wants to accomplish.

Tell your loved one how much you care and encourage him/her to call you for moral support. Make it clear to him/her, that as much as you would like to, you will NOT give him/her money. You can offer food or pay a bill yourself, but you cannot give cash or anything that can be converted to cash.[*Hint:* Gift cards can be traded on the street for dope or cash.]

Get in touch with AL-ANON and allow it to help guide you. There are also other organizations; then pray everyday for self control and wisdom for you and for strength for your loved one. As you pray, realize that you need healing as much as your loved one and understand that, paradoxically, the only way that you heal together is to each heal separately.

Always remember that recovery is not an event, it is a journey. I wish you luck. May God bless your family and you on your journey.

CHAPTER 37

YOUNG PUNKS

To all you young punks out there, let me give you something to think about. Why have you never heard of such a thing as "old punks"?

Clint Eastwood as Dirty Harry: "…you've gotta ask yourself a question, do I feel lucky? Well, do ya, punk?"

Of late, there is a new breed on the street, younger, more violent, and too immature to understand just how stupid they appear, even to the more seasoned drug addicts who look down on them as fools.

These punks smoke and peddle crystal meth, thinking they are tough, smart, and attractive to the girls who hang around them. If you are one of these punks, the girls are with you for your dope, nothing else and nothing more. You bring nothing to the table other than your dope and your idiotic attitude which will get your ass kicked on the street.

Some of these punks still look at   first razor longingly, dreaming of the day when they might need to use it, but they strut around like they are "da man." They grew up on violent video games wherein people got shot or stabbed and popped up again when they hit the reset button or the backspace key.

They do not have the first clue that they are destroying their lives and the lives of the people whom they supply. They don't care because these fools think that life has a reset button just like their video games.

So, they give no thought to whipping out a machete and swinging it at somebody. They don't understand how the street works and when they pull one of their blades on, or beak off to, the wrong person they will be eating their weapons for lunch and their tough-guy words will still be lodged in their throat.

The dealers who supply them mostly laugh at them. These youngsters are failures in school, at any kind of athletics, and destined to be failures in life if they don't get their shit in one sock, very soon. They think being a dope dealer makes them cool. It doesn't; it just brings them short term excitement and substitutes for self respect.

They won't come at you face to face, but don't turn your back on them. They are only dangerous because of crystal meth courage that makes them unpredictable and eager to earn their street creds by some act of violence.

According to www.drugfreeamerica.org, meth is commonly manufactured in illegal, hidden laboratories, mixing various forms of amphetamine (another stimulant drug) or derivatives with other chemicals to boost its potency. Common pills for cold remedies are often used as the basis for the production of the drug. The meth "cook" extracts ingredients from those pills, and to increase its strength, combines the substance with chemicals such as battery acid, drain cleaner, lantern fuel, and antifreeze. It is highly addictive and gives a relatively, at least monetarily speaking, cheap high.

Most of these punks sell crystal meth, AKA: shard, side, ice, crystal, or just meth. You may have already seen the pictures that follow this page, but even if you have, they are worth looking at again because this is what you are smoking, injecting, or swallowing and it is what you are selling to your friends and your custies.

The pictures are time-lapse photography of various addicts and are taken from their mug shots. Take a good look because if you continue using this shit, the pictures represent your destiny.

If you have a child, these are the pictures that your child sees in his/her nightmares. You are creating those nightmares.

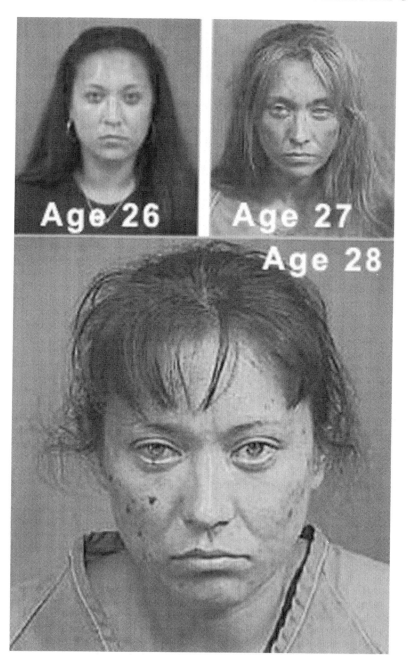

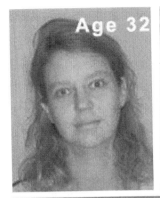
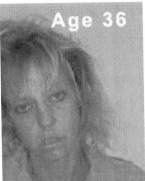
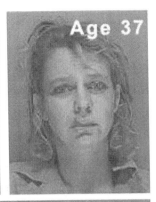

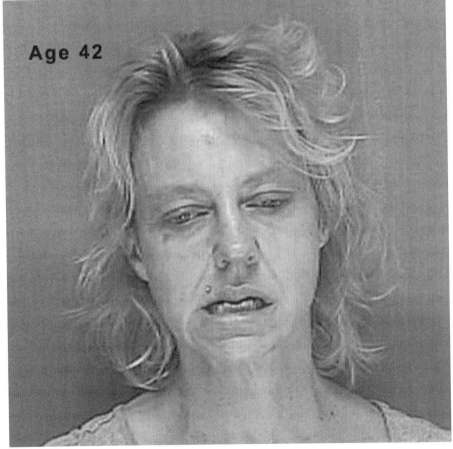

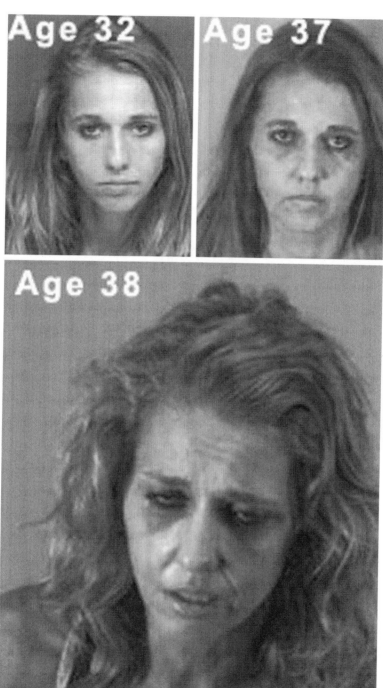

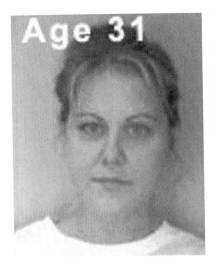

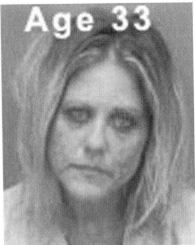

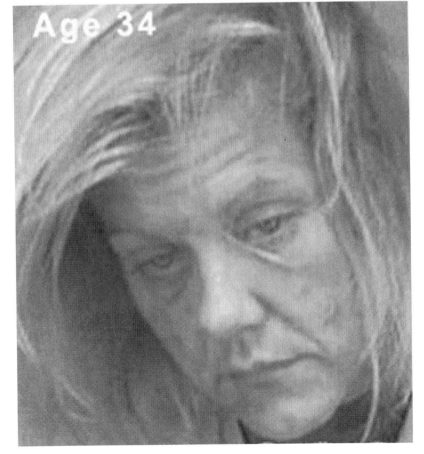

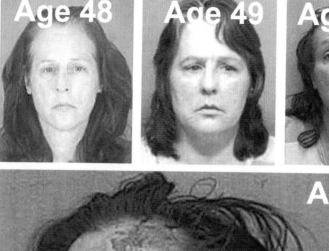

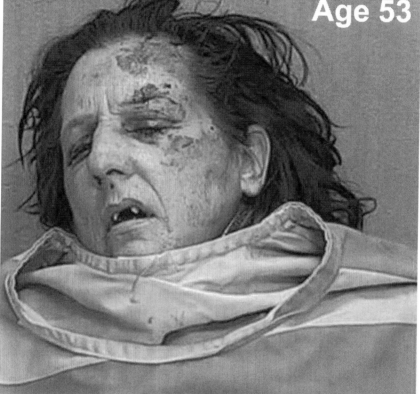

How cool do you think you are now, asshole? How cool do you think you will be in a few years?

I'll tell you how cool you will be. If you go to jail before you end up looking like one of the pictures above, you'll be the youngest, prettiest thing in the cell block.

Do you know what happens to young, pretty things in jail? Let's just put it this way, if you were a football player when you went in, no matter what position you played, guard, tackle, maybe tight end, you're going to come out of prison a "wide receiver."

CHAPTER 38

HOW TO DEFEAT ILLEGAL DRUGS

Approximately 550 people per year are murdered in Canada. About 325 people per year die of drug overdoses just in Vancouver alone.

Is it not obvious to you that drug dealers are murderers and that drug dealers kill far more people with their drugs than all the other forms of murder combined? So why are we treating drug dealers like petty criminals?

Sun Tzu, The Art of War: "Strategy without tactics is the slowest route to victory. Tactics without strategy is the noise before defeat."

The police are fighting Canada's war on drugs without the help of the laws, absent the help of politicians who make the laws, and with precious little support from the courts. Under these conditions, there is no long term plan possible, meaning that we are demanding that our police fight only a series of battles, rather than a strategic war

They are being asked to win a war wherein they are not provided the tools needed to gain victory. This strategy, as it exists, is absurd until all levels of government pull together and make a conscientious effort to execute a coordinated strategy. Here is a war plan that allows our police to be proactive rather than simply reactive.

Almost all non-spontaneous criminal activity is about the risk/reward ratio; if the risk is too great, versus the reward, most criminals will commit a less risky crime. Accordingly, as selling drugs is a non-spontaneous criminal activity the risk/reward ratio must be attacked to halt the spread of drugs and to stop the proliferation of the gangs built upon the distribution of drugs.

The reward portion of the risk/reward ratio is unassailable, because the only way in which drugs go down in street value, and therefore profit potential, is to flood the market with them. Accordingly, it is apparent that the risk factor must be attacked in order to achieve any success in controlling the proliferation of drugs.

There are two methods by which to increase the risk factor. The first is to virtually guarantee criminals that they will get caught if they are involved in the drug trade. That is already the situation as was proven in other chapters in this book; almost all dealers at any level of the distribution chain eventually get caught by the police.

Accordingly, it is obvious that the current punishment for getting caught is not viewed by the dealers (gangster and otherwise) as adverse enough to the risk/reward factor to cause them to quit dealing; otherwise the guarantee of getting caught, in and of itself, would have stopped, if not at least slowed, the proliferation of drugs in general.

Understanding that, it is evident that a second dynamic must be brought to bear on the risk factor. The second way to render the risk/reward ratio too steep for the majority of criminals is to make the penalty so severe for being involved in any particular crime that the penalty alone throws the risk/reward ratio out of whack for the average criminal.

That logic leads to the inescapable conclusion that the laws and the courts, not the police, are the weak links, and therefore bear a substantial fault for our current situation with drugs because the police have no control over the penalties. The job of the police is simply to recognize criminal activity and then to arrest those responsible for that activity. It is the laws and the courts that determine the penalties, and thereby have the power to discourage any particular criminal activity by altering the risk/reward ratio.

In making the determination as to which criminal activity should receive the longest sentences, the laws and the courts must decide which criminal activities are the most odious or put society at the greatest risk, and assign the strongest penalty to those particular criminal activities.

That being understood, and focusing attention herein only on illegal drugs, if society wants to get control of the drug problem, the laws and the courts need to recognize that all drugs are not created equal, that some drugs have more destructive properties than others, and therefore, have the potential to harm society to a greater degree. In keeping with this principle, the punishment for being involved with those more insidious and sinister drugs needs to be greater than the punishment for being involved with other illegal drugs.

Throwing a "one size covers all" approach at the drug scene guarantees failure as it does not allow for the targeting of specific drugs. The laws and the courts must also recognize which drugs should be the priority and to assign that priority based, not only on the potential harm to society of a particular drug, but also based upon how deeply entrenched within society any drug might be at the present. This harm-versus-entrenchment analysis will determine the need for priority removal of any particular drug(s) and the possible success rate at removing that drug from the drug scene, and thereby create an order as to which drug(s) to attack first.

The Criminal Code of Canada has long recognized that certain crimes should come with stiffer penalties than others because of the severity of those crimes, because of the damage done by those crimes, or because of what the details of any of those crimes might reveal about the mindset of the offender. For instance, it would be considered silly to sentence a shoplifter to the same time in jail as, say, a burglar, who stealthily violates the sanctity of an individual's home, or a robber who enters an individual's residence under force and employs a weapon to do so.

In the same manner in which the justice system currently classifies various criminal acts as more heinous than others and recognizes those differences by imposing greater sentences, depending on the criminal act, the sale of certain drugs needs to carry a more severe penalty than the sale of other drugs.

There is little doubt that cocaine and heroin are deeply entrenched at almost all levels of society, meaning that they will be the most difficult of the main three drugs (cocaine, heroin and crystal meth) to eradicate. Therefore, without advocating the use or sale of cocaine or heroin, the system needs to deal first with crystal meth and with illegally manufactured designer drugs falling under the umbrella of crystal meth, drugs such as ecstasy and bath salts.

The bath salts spoken of here are not your grandmother's bath salts, but like crystal meth are another amphetamine based designer drug packaged to attract our youth, and according to medical authorities, more addictive than cocaine and ten times more dangerous.

Even a cursory glance at the pictures in the previous chapter should make it absolutely clear to you that crystal meth is far and away the most dangerous of the three main drugs most commonly in use by addicts, and those pictures do not speak to the many dangers of manufacturing, the added risk to the police of busting a crystal meth lab because of the explosive properties inherent in the manufacturing chemicals, and the poison gasses produced by those processes, nor show the added desperation and rage of crystal meth users compared with those who use only heroin and/or cocaine.

Because crystal meth is by far the most insidious of the big three drugs, as well as being the newest drug among them, and therefore, less entrenched in society, it follows that crystal meth should be the priority target. Accordingly, the manufacture of crystal meth, the possession of it for the purpose of trafficking, the simple possession of it, or the simple use of it, should bring the most severe sentences compared to any of the other drugs, thereby attacking it at all four tiers of the drug chain: user, user-dealer and nonuser-dealer, distributor, and manufacturer.

Absent this "all-tiers" approach, any program that attempts to eradicate crystal meth will be virtually useless because any tier(s) not attacked will give rise to those in the remaining tiers seeing a reason to continue to be involved with crystal meth and those involved in those unattacked tiers will rise up and fill the void in any tier(s) that, theretofore, might have been successfully eliminated.

Before offering a complete solution though, first examine the two different types of drug dealers who exist, user-dealer and nonuser-dealers, and realize how critical the differentiation between the two categories is to finding a solution the current drug problem.

Examining the nonuser-dealers, these individuals sell for pure greed. It is all about the money to them, and therefore, their business model is one that seeks to expand the territories which they service in order to grow their profitability. In their drive to enlarge their territories, they often employ brutal tactics to intimidate and wipe out non-gang-affiliated dealers, as well as become involved in gang wars with competing gangs, all in an effort to seek to ensure that all drugs are purchased from them.

Additionally, no gang wants to allow a lone wolf to pop up in its territory and cut the gang's profit. Therefore, the lone-wolf dealer, if lucky, will be given the choice of joining the gang or suffering the consequences. But more often, will be unlucky and will simply be pushed out under a threat of a death, a warning about which often comes with a severe beating.

When gangs decide to invade a new territory, they will employ the same brutal tactics as they use to hold a territory to establish that territory and solidify their hold on it. When moving into a new territory though, existing nonuser-dealers within that territory are often recruited. That analysis reveals the nonuser-dealers pose the greatest threat to society.

The nonuser-dealers are also, by far, the more odious of two categories of dealers, user-dealer versus nonuser-dealer, because nonuser-dealers are purposely taking advantage of the addicts, people whom they probably hold in low regard.

On the other hand, the user-dealer is selling principally to support an addiction. The user-dealers might grow the number of addicts they service, but will never vastly expand a territory because the user-dealers are also doing dope and will almost always expand their personal addictions to the point that they will put themselves out of business, either by having no time to expand because of their addiction(s) or because they will attract so much attention through carelessness brought about by their addictions that they get caught and end up in jail for a long enough period of time to force them to start their business over from scratch each time they might be released.

Thus, user-dealers are already victims of their addiction(s), and as such, are their own worst enemies. Accordingly, it makes little sense to allocate any significant importance to most user-dealers, especially early on the battle plan. Additionally, the carelessly overt activities of the user-dealer mean that user-dealers will be easier to follow, giving the police an avenue with which to identify the drug supply chain that will always lead

to nonuser-dealers, and then distributors, and eventually to manufacturers.
While this conversation is about crystal meth only, the tactics employed can
also be successfully implemented when the time arrives to target cocaine
and/or heroin.

None of the above excuses user-dealers from the criminality of their
actions, but they are mitigating factors that should be considered within the
law and/or at sentencing. Additionally, these factors need to be considered
and understood in order to develop an effective overall plan for eliminating
crystal meth, and eventually other drugs.

Factoring in the differences between nonuser-dealers and user-dealers
with their different motivations in dealing, it becomes apparent that a
society free from nonuser-dealers will likely be a less violent society, a society
with fewer drug problems, and a society with fewer gangs, and therefore,
a society that can then concentrate more of its resources on working with
addicts instead of incarcerating them.

The laws and the courts need to recognize the larger threat to society
created by nonuser-dealers and the different intentions of the nonuser-
dealers, versus the user-dealers.

.Considering the addiction versus non-addiction of a dealer is similar
to considering the mindset of an individual who punches somebody.
Was that individual punching largely unprovoked in order to inflict the
maximum damage possible, or was that individual punching simply as a
knee jerk reaction out of a sudden anger? The law, especially at sentencing,
recognizes a difference.

Accordingly, the statutes should create different statutes for nonuser-
dealers versus user-dealers. Manslaughter and murder, although both are
homicides, are different statutes and recognize intentions as the only thing
separating one of those crimes from the other. Thus, this proposal is in
keeping with current legal principles.

Prior to the enactment of statutes that differentiate user-dealers from
nonuser-dealers, the courts can still have a significant, if not decisive,
impact through their sentencing standards, given the wide range of possible
sentences available to them under their judicial authority and discretion.

If the actual laws are not going to specify a difference between the
nonuser-dealer and the user-dealer, then it is up to the courts to create
a distinction via their sentencing standards, giving nonuser-dealers much
more severe sentences than user-dealers.

In addition to sentencing standards, the courts also have another tool available to them to discourage crystal meth sales and drug sales, in general, by nonuser-dealers: bail. The bail argument is simple; bail is principally granted or denied based on the threat to society presented by the accused.

The analysis has, thus far, clearly demonstrated that crystal meth is a danger to society beyond other drugs and that the nonuser-dealer is a greater risk to society than the user-dealer. Accordingly, society requires added protection from nonuser-dealers and from those who sell crystal meth. That added protection can come not just at sentencing, but also earlier in the process in the form of not granting bail.

From the criminal's viewpoint, not granting bail also has a negative effect on the risk/reward ratio. Currently, after being caught, a drug dealer will delay the trial for as long as possible, sometimes up to two years or more, thus delaying punishment.

This ability to delay punishment causes the laws to lose their deterentcy value because drug dealers, at least in their minds, are free to go about their activities for the foreseeable future with almost no repercussions. On the other hand, were there to be a denial of bail, those caught dealing would have an incentive to have their trial as soon as possible because they would be stuck in jail awaiting trial.

So, a "no bail" position by the courts brings the following benefits.

1. It protects the public.
2. It pulls the offenders from the street where they will not be committing more crimes and costing the system even more money.
3. It serves to reinforce the deterentcy value of the laws.
4. It speeds the process through the court system, saving time, and therefore, money.
5. As well, giving the nonuser-dealer a much stiffer sentence has a myriad of benefits to society and to the war on drugs.
6. With stiffer sentences for nonuser-dealers, gangs are somewhat discouraged because many nonuser-dealers have gang affiliations or buy from gangs.
7. With stiffer sentences for nonuser-dealers, when gangs do deal and get caught, those gang members will be in prison longer.
8. With stiffer sentences for nonuser-dealers, our youth will be less inclined to join a gang because the riches will come less quickly and with greater risks.
9. With stiffer sentences for nonuser-dealers, nonuser-dealers will

need to find user-dealers to run their drugs for them, cutting their ability to make a profit as user-dealers will be far less dependable workers, while posing a variety of other previously discussed risks to the nonuser-dealer.

10. With stiffer sentences for nonuser-dealers, the police will have a greater incentive to focus their attentions on the nonuser-dealer because that will be the most effective way for the police to control drug activity, thereby assuring the most effective use of the police.

11. With stiffer sentences for nonuser-dealers, the police will have another tool with which to prosecute gangs without the need positively to prove gang affiliation or organized crime.

12. With police then targeting nonuser-dealers, police will more effectively identify the nonuser-dealers because user-dealers, due to their addiction(s), are somewhat more careless than nonuser-dealers, and therefore the user-dealers will lead police to the nonuser-dealers.

13. Additionally, the police will automatically concentrate their efforts on crystal meth and nonuser-dealers because, by comparative, it is more rewarding from a police perspective to catch a robber than a shoplifter.

14. Another ancillary benefit to police is that the current "catch and release" attitude of the courts is a morale killer to their rank and file. Police are a force comprised of individuals who, for the most part, are dedicated to their jobs, wanting to do those jobs to the best of their abilities. The current revolving door for drug dealers, in and out of custody, is a morale buster to many of them. They often catch the same drug dealer three or four times within a month because the courts continually release that dealer. If I was a cop, I would wonder why I bothered to catch the guy in the first place.

15. A final benefit is that with stiffer sentences, more users will be willing to cooperate with police in furthering police investigations in the hope that cooperation might lead to a reduced sentence.

Given this proposed new law or sentencing standard, the problem would arise as to how the police could prove the difference between a nonuser-dealer and a user-dealer. The principle for the solution also already exists in current law.

Under current drunk-driving statutes, an individual is charged with an offense equal to drunk driving for refusing to submit to an intoxication test.

Therefore, as police have a duty to provide care to any individual in their custody, police might be allowed or even required to administer some sort of drug test in order to adequately determine if any individuals arrested while in possession of drugs needs to be observed for that individual's own safety, in case of possible adverse reactions to any controlled substances they might have ingested or otherwise used.

Under this protocol and with more severe sentences for nonuser-dealers, versus user-dealers, any individuals charged with possession could be required to give a urine sample, or submit to a blood test which checks for the presence of the drug(s) of which they are in possession. These tests, when done through a urine sample, can yield a conclusive result within minutes and the equipment and expertise required to administer them is absolutely minimum.

Then, for example, if any individuals are caught with both cocaine and heroin, sufficient enough in amount to be considered "possession for the purpose of selling," those individuals will need to test positive for the use of both drugs or be charged as a nonuser-dealer for any drug(s) which they possessed, but which the test found them not to be using.

If this objective of forcing the administration of a drug test is not accomplishable by police protocol, then it could certainly be accomplished by a statute similar to drunk-driving statutes, wherein any individuals refusing an alcohol sobriety test are automatically guilty of a charge, the sentence for which is equal to that of an individual having failed the alcohol sobriety test.

Accordingly, any drug arrestee refusing the drug use test would automatically be guilty of refusing a lawful test and subject to the stiffer penalties of a nonuser-dealer versus a user-dealer, and the trafficking charge would be dropped. If this can be done to stop drunken driving, one should certainly be able to apply an equal solution to drug dealing, a crime which incontestably does more damage to society, as well as impairs those operating a motor vehicle.

As previously stated, if the police are to be able to perform the duties that the citizens ask of them, the police must be given the tools needed to accomplish their duties. If not, the laws and the courts are failing the police, not visa versa, and the price to be paid for this failure is the proliferation of gangs and gang violence, as well as all the ancillary problems that come with such, even more drugs, even more guns, and even more property crime, etc.

For this differentiation of sentences to be an effective deterrent, and for the sake of justice, the time to which a nonuser-dealer gets sentenced must be substantially more than that of the user-dealer. If there is not a substantial difference, there will not be a substantial deterrent.

A suggested minimum of five years for a nonuser-dealer with the refusal to submit to a drug test also being penalized with five years, thus eliminating the need to prove the original drug charge(s) if the drug test is refused, would seem an effective level of punishment and deterrence while still serving the needs of justice.

Returning our focus to the various drugs now, without proposing it, but only to prove a point by an example, how many crystal meth users would there be if the sentence for using it was life in prison? The answer is obviously, very few.

It needs to be understood that crystal meth has altered the landscape as far as drugs go and that other future chemical creations might carry the same, or worse, characteristics. In fact, there are many other concoctions that are starting to become more and more prevalent, drugs such as rhino, frenzy, bubbles, etc. For the user, crystal meth and these other designer drugs are a cheaper high that lasts longer than highs from other drugs. For the small-time dealer, these are more profitable and easier to procure.

For the manufacturer, they are wildly more profitable and avoid having to smuggle drugs across the border because they can be manufactured anywhere, using common ingredients found at most hardware stores and drug stores.

For society, and for the police, they are far more dangerous because of the increased violence and paranoia associated with their use and the dangers from poisonous gasses and explosions inherent in their manufacture, processes that can occur next door to you or even to a school.

That being the case and starting with the principle that one cannot effectively drive a railroad spike with a tack hammer, society needs to ask itself how motivated it is to eradicate crystal meth and other designer drugs from the drugs commonly found on the street.

It seems obvious that eliminating these drugs is an absolute imperative because their march through society must be halted before they poison more children and inexorably alter the level of violence from the drug community in general. So, if the police are to be permitted to be fully successful, the solution being sought is a penalty that decisively skews the risk reward/ratio against each link of the crystal meth and designer drug chain, while still serving the need for justice.

Suggested Penalties for Crystal Meth & Designer Drugs
Manufacturer: 7 to 10 years

This sentence recognizes the damage done to society by manufacturing these drugs, and the callousness of the individual(s) toward the safety of citizens and the safety of our police due to the dangers of the lab in which they are made.

Nonuser-dealer: 5 to 7 years.

This sentence recognizes the absolute lack of personal concern of the individual in dealing such a dangerous and destructive drug for pure avarice.

User-dealer: 3 to 4 years.

This sentence, while still in keeping with skewing the risk/reward ratio, provides a measure of leniency, due to the fact that the individual is supporting a habit in this case. (This sentence should warn him/her to find a different addiction).

User: 2 years (Upon 2nd offense).

This sentence, while not an attempt to punish the addict because addicts spend most of their time punishing themselves, might at first glance seem severe, but it is necessary to encourage addicts to use something other than crystal meth, thereby stopping demand for the drug. It also gives the addict a very fair start on kicking his/her crystal meth addiction, either before getting caught a second time, or in jail if he/she does not switch his/her drug of choice after getting caught the first time.

Even should you believe that this new risk/reward ratio will not stop the upper-level drug lords from dealing crystal meth and its ilk because those individuals are too protected to reach, it will still succeed because you have failed to factor in that unless those upper-level drug dealers can find foot soldiers to deliver their designer drugs, there will be no profit for them in its manufacture. Accordingly, the risk/reward ratio defeats crystal meth and its ilk anyhow because the small guys (foot soldiers) are not going to risk a long jail sentence with these drugs when they could deal other illegal drugs and incur far less risk.

Again, the solution being offered is for crystal meth and its ilk, as opposed to cocaine and heroin. It would be foolhardy to apply this solution to all three major drugs at once as part of the success of this plan is to make the use or sale of heroin or cocaine a preferable choice to all who might be involved with crystal meth, at any level. Remember the words of Sun Tzu in The Art of War, "*Build your opponent a golden bridge to retreat across.*"

Recognizing that a drug addict will find a drug to use, this is not an attempt to wipe out drug use, and will sputter if that is how it is implemented; it is a plan to wipe out the most insidious of the drugs, namely crystal meth and its ilk. Thus, it is a strategy that will recoup society's losses in the current drug war by returning to the days before dangerous chemical concoctions. Only after regaining the ground already lost because of them will it be possible to go after the other drugs and actually start gaining ground in this battle with drugs.

Lawmakers, politicians, and every citizen need to come together on this issue and give the police the opportunity to be as effective as possible in this campaign If you are of the same mind, let your voices be heard. Call your MLAs and MPs, write letters to the editors of newspapers, and get your friends involved in promoting this solution.

If you agree with the reasoning above, then take things one step further. Don't just stamp out crystal meth and its current ilk; but instead, also anticipate the arrival of new drugs on the scene, possibly more chemists' concoctions of the future, and possibly the arrival on the drug scene of other organic hallucinogens from whatever country of origin.

A possible law might have wording to the effect of: "…the possession of any drug or substance, unless specifically prescribed by a medical doctor and not already falling under the Controlled Drug and Substances Act, that alters users' perceptions when smoked, ingested, absorbed by the skin, injected or otherwise introduced to the human body, whether that drug or substance is organic and/or chemical and whether or not that drug or substance is labeled for human consumption, if the person in possession of that drug or substance cannot demonstrate a legitimate need for veterinary purposes." All drugs or substances falling under the purview of this new law would be treated under the law(s) as though they are crystal meth.

Society cannot afford to allow a new drug to creep into the market and enrich the coffers of gangs because the laws failed to anticipate a particular chemical formula, or because nobody could have reasonably been aware of some organic compound's hallucinogenic effects, and therefore its imminent importation and use.

With the correct laws defining what is a controlled substance, there is an opportunity to confine the main problem to cocaine and heroin, products over which, although harmful and pervasive, an infrastructure as well as considerable intelligence already exists with which to combat its spread once the drug problem has been largely limited to those substances.

At first glance, this may seem counterintuitive; but, by employing a "high penalty" strategy against all substances other than cocaine and heroin, law enforcement can eliminate those other substances as a problem, or a potential problem, before their use becomes dominant, thus providing for better control of cocaine and heroin in the future. Once all other substances have been contained, law enforcement can more freely focus its attention on cocaine and heroin.

Again, the "high penalty" strategy will be effective because it attacks all levels of the drug chain: manufacturer, user-dealer, nonuser-dealer, and the gang component, with that gang component being a cornerstone in any distribution chain dealing with drugs. This is not a legalization of cocaine and heroin and is not even a decriminalization of those two substances.

The suggested strategy is similar to a country focusing on cutting off the supply line and interrupting the recruitment process for any opposing army before turning its full attention to the ground troops. Think of cocaine and heroin as the ground troops of an opposing army, and of all other drugs as the supply line and the recruitment tools for dealers and gang bangers.

Such an approach would not be met with a criticism saying that nobody was concerned with the ground troops. It would be understood that without fresh supplies and without fresh recruits, the opposing army would soon be relegated to insignificance.

Finally, any discussion of more severe laws is pointless if that discussion fails to address the most critical arrow in the quiver of society to allow it to win this battle with nonuser-dealers and with crystal meth and its ilk, namely, the courts. The justices must be on board with this strategy or it is doomed to failure, because without the justices on board, there is bark, but no bite; and a dog without teeth will always go hungry.

With the justices on board, even absent new laws, much can be done to discourage crystal meth and its ilk. I do not know if the laws should impose whatever sentencing standards might evolve from this idea with "mandatory minimums" or how the battle plan brings aboard the cooperation of the courts, I just know that the courts must also aggressively support the police in this effort if success is to be achieved.

How can such a plan be budgeted? I am not a CEO of anything right now, but I do have considerable experience, having started some dozen businesses over the years, with one of them doing over $2,000,000 in sales its second year and $4,000,000 in its third year, before I sold it. That experience tells me that an aggressive program such as the one outlined above would actually save money, not cost more money.

Of course, incarceration costs would increase, but offsetting that would be the saving in multiple areas.

1.   There would be less money spent on police investigations because the individuals who are in jail for being involved with crystal meth and nonuser-dealers will not be released for many years, thus slowing the revolving door.

2.   Also offsetting those incarceration costs would be the fact that there would be fewer court appearances by dealers because they would be in jail longer, where they would be unable to sling or commit other crimes.

3.   Further offsetting these incarceration costs would be the lack of need to spend large sums to prove gang affiliation because the sentences would be tantamount to being sentenced as a gang member.

Frankly, the courts seem deficient in doing their job even with the laws that currently exist. Most sentences, at least here in BC, lend themselves to being medium to lenient sentences, with those sentences generally being considerably lighter here than in other jurisdictions, demanding convictions on a significant number of similar charges before the courts even consider a sentence that might actually be severe enough to serve as a deterrent.

This leniency creates an additional problem because criminals will always migrate to any area in which, if caught, their crime will be treated with the most leniency. It's the risk/reward ratio that was addressed earlier.

Thus, an invitation has been issued to deal drugs here with the promise that the punishment for doing so will be inconsequential when compared to other jurisdictions, thereby also issuing an invitation to gangs.

The courts need immediately to start handing out maximum sentences for drug violations involving all drugs with the exception of user-dealer sales of cocaine and heroin. Remember, if you buy into this strategy, the goal is first to eliminate all the other drugs and the nonuser-dealers.

Finally, it seems prudent that the illicit sale of prescription pills should fall under the "all other drugs" umbrella, thereby further choking off the profit potential of the gangs, and in the process discouraging the growth of the illegal prescription pill industry.

It is inarguable that those who sell prescription pills and other controlled medicines are doing so not only at a cost to society by the destructive power of those substances when improperly used, but are also stealing from the healthcare system because it is almost an inescapable conclusion that the healthcare system originally provided those drugs at a monetary cost to every citizen.

Additionally, all too often those prescription drugs find there way south of our border, where they are traded for weapons, other drugs, or cash with which to build more crystal meth labs or import more guns.

The fraudulent cost to the healthcare system of this diversion of medicines impacts the healthcare system's ability to render services to those who really need medicines and who would benefit from care not being delayed due to budgetary considerations. Thus, the illegal sale of prescription drugs, as some might like to say, is not a victimless crime. Every citizen is actually a victim.

This last fact alone should be enough to justify the inclusion of such prescription drugs among those substances that need to qualify for a higher penalty when illegally sold and/or procured outside of legal channels.

The solutions, discussed herein, cannot wait because with every delay the enemy is inflicting more damage and strengthening its position. With every delay more citizens are at risk. Action needs to be taken NOW!

The bottom line here is this: criminals will always fear the cops because they do not want to get caught, but if any crime is to be abated, the criminals need to fear the courts as much as the cops, if not more.

Why this plan? You will often hear the argument from nonuser-dealers that they are only there to fill a need and that they wouldn't be slinging if there weren't any addicts. Of course, the counter argument to that is there wouldn't be any addicts if there weren't any dealers to supply them. It's the old chicken–and-egg argument.

If you really want to know which came first though, it was the dope, so it is ignorant and counterproductive to become caught up in this silly argument that really makes no difference because solving a philosophical issue will do nothing to eradicate the drug problem in today's society.

The facts are, as was proven, that if society wants to take the biggest bite out of the drug problem, the nonuser-dealers and the most harmful drugs must be targeted first.

END OF CHAPTER QUESTION

22. Do you agree with the sentencing principles in this chapter?

Post your answer on www.breakingthecode.ca.

EPILOGUE

Winston Churchill: **"All the great things are simple, and many can be expressed in a single word: freedom, justice, honor, duty, mercy, hope."**

Democritus: **"By desiring little, a poor man makes himself rich."**

A few years ago, when my roommate and I lived outside of the downtown area, we had grown accustomed to seeing an old bum pushing his shopping cart full of treasures up and down the main road. It seemed to us as though he had no place to go and wasn't in a hurry to get there because he would be headed along going one direction and an hour later we might see him struggling with his cart going the opposite direction.

He was probably in his sixties, or close thereto, but because of the gray, wiry beard that covered most of his face and the wear from the street and the weather that masked the rest of his face, it was difficult to know.

He was definitely overweight, even rotund, wearing an old, dirt worn, green, nylon jacket that flapped open at the bottom where a zipper should have held it together. His pants were khaki-esque or what I might describe as a "smudgy street brown." He had on an old pair of boots, scuffed but looking functional, military style, gaping open because of no laces, and he shuffled rather than walked making it appear as if the boots were heavier than he could handle.

Anyhow, it was a few days before Christmas and my roommate and I were returning from Costco, having bought some gifts for her family, when we spotted this old guy walking his usual route. Wanting to teach my roommate a lesson about the true joy that can come from giving, I pulled over the car a half a block or so ahead of him, handed her a fifty dollar bill and told her that we should walk back and give it to the old guy, that it might be the best gift he ever received and that we ever received.

We exited the vehicle, walked the few yards back to him and my roommate extended her hand to him with the fifty dollar bill in it and said words to the effect of, "Please take this and enjoy your Christmas; we want you to treat yourself."

The elderly guy then shocked us both by declining the money and extracting a fifty dollar bill of his own from his pocket, saying, "Thank you, but I don't need the money; I am happy and have money of my own. Somebody else gave me fifty dollars the other day and I don't know what to do with it."

That old guy, at least in my mind, had gone from being a bum on the street for whom I had felt sorry, to being a man, but not just a man, an actual gentleman, and a gentleman of honor. In the course of some twenty seconds, he had reminded me of a lesson that I had learned years ago, a lesson about judging a book by its cover, and he did it in a way that still makes me smile and cry at the same time every time I think of him. I was, and am, humbled by the caliber of that gentleman.

About a week later when we had not seen him for awhile, I stopped at a gas station along his usual route and inquired about him. The young lady behind the counter told me that he had passed away a few days prior, that he was lying next to his shopping cart when he was found.

It saddened me, but I take comfort in knowing that he had found contentment, despite his lot in life. To all you people out there who think life is hopeless, remember that old gentleman, and remember how little he had and how little it took for him to be content, and then take comfort in what you have and move on doing the right thing with your life if you want more or want to change it.

Honor his memory and what he taught us. Be as much of a man as that old gentleman and you can also find contentment.

GLOSSARY OF TERMS

Break	Score a paying date
Crack	Rock cocaine
Deep Six	Really undercover cop/car
Down	Heroin, any opiate or opioid
Goof	One who talks to guards in jail
Hoop	Secret dope or money up an orifice
Hoot	Decent sized drag of crack
Jugger	One who injects in their neck
Meth	Crystal meth
Mook	Just a nobody or a guy off the street
Needler	One who injects drugs
Pants	Heroin, any opiate or opioid
Push a Pipe	To scrape the cocaine residue from the inside of a crack pipe so it can be smoked and not wasted
Rat	One who talks to the police
Rail	Line of powdered cocaine for snorting
Rig	Hypodermic needle, or the act of injecting drugs
Shirts	Cocaine powdered or rock
Shit your bed	Use all your dope that was for sale
Side	Crystal meth, AKA: shard
Six	Police
Six Under	Undercover police car/person
Six Up	Marked police car
Smash	To inject dope
Speedball	Injected mix of cocaine & heroin
Teching	The compulsive act of fiddling with something
Ten-Ten	No wants or warrants
Toke	Small drag of crack
Up	Cocainet

APPENDIX

Check out your landlord as carefully as he supposedly checks you out.

Desiderius Erasmus: "He who allows oppression shares the crime."

Several months after having moved into the Douglas Manor Apartments, a former fleabag motel converted into studio apartments by a simple stroke of a pen, a contractor, Jaime Peddle of Peddle Construction, showed up purporting himself to be one of the owners, and announcing to the tenants and to the various City Planning review boards how he was going to upgrade all the units and offer current tenants the opportunity to occupy the soon-to-be renovated units.

Previously, the owner and resident manager had been accepting, even soliciting, those on welfare, as well as otherwise challenged individuals to become tenants. Peddle, despite his announcement, and in an obvious attempt to start with a fresh slate of tenants, quickly thereafter began evicting tenants right and left.

Soon Peddle began having his manager hand out rent receipts on scraps of paper instead of from a numbered receipt pad. It is difficult for anybody to do a proper audit of books with such a rent collection policy causing one to wonder why a supposedly legitimate enterprise would resort to such a business practice when a proper receipt book costs less than five dollars at the local Staples office supply store.

Peddle attempted, on at least four occasions, to evict my roommate and me. On one occasion, the Residential Tenancy Branch actually ruled in his favor, but I quickly had that ruling overturned, because the RTB determined that it was obtained by fraud.

Understanding what Peddle was up to, I began helping other tenants whom Peddle was trying to evict, successfully fighting off many of Peddle's actions. Then one day, every tenant received a notice on their door stating that the building had been issued a building permit for renovations, and as permitted under the Residential Tenancy Act, everybody was being evicted.

I immediately spoke with a City Counselor and went to the City Planning Commission where I determined that the only problem with this supposed building permit allowing the evictions sought by Peddle was that it didn't exist, it was a subterfuge to trick tenants into vacating their apartments and their rights. I was able to successfully prove to many of the tenants that Peddle was lying about having a building permit, but not before a large percentage of the tenants just gave up and moved.

Peddle ran a heavy handed operation, proclaiming to the police and to the RTB that he was an owner and then built on his supposed ownership and his lies about having a building permit, using whatever ruses he could to attempt to get tenants to move out. He even moved in a friend of his next door to me in an attempt to intimidate other tenants and me. His friend would stand outside his apartment and drink beer half the night while making snide and offensive remarks to other tenants, to my roommate, and to me.

In turn, I contacted the police, the city, the newspapers and the radio stations with the truth, resulting in the police, refusing to allow a representative to any of the arbitration hearing to back up Peddle, and generating various newspaper articles and a radio interview. Peddle had actually gone to the extent of allowing toxic black mould to infest the building.

I filed with the RTB complaining about the health risks to other tenants and to me, and Peddle claimed he had remediated the mould. I then took pictures and presented them to RTB proving that either Peddle lied about having remediated the mould or that Peddle Construction had done such a shoddy job fixing the problem that the mould seemed to be continuing to grow unabated. Even though Peddle fought that submission by me, he lost the arbitration hearing and was ordered to clean up the problem.

These arbitration hearing are held over the telephone as a conference call, thus no participant can see another participant. I remember one particular hearing in which Peddle was trying to have my roommate and me evicted. I was sixty-six years old at the time and played the "senior card" telling the arbitrator that Peddle was trying to push around a senior citizen. Peddle responded with words to the effect of, "He may be sixty-six, but he's like no sixty-six year old you have ever met." I still chuckle today when I think of that hearing. By the way, we won.

With Peddle's ruthless tactics exposed and him losing so many eviction hearings, he then disconnected everybody's cable television and internet (services that had theretofore been included as part of the rental package), and sometime later turned off water service and even electric service. Peddle was relentless in his pursuit of violating tenant rights.

These maneuvers forced all but a few of the remaining residents to move out, but not before many of them were awarded thousands of dollars via mediation within the legal system. I fought this fight with those tenants, helping them with their paperwork, because one cannot allow an injustice to occur if one has the ability to stop it.

Today I see that Douglas Manor is being renovated and Peddle has a sign for his construction company on the fence out front, proclaiming his company's slogan, "Rock Solid." To this sign, I remind people that limestone is also a rock, but it crumbles under pressure. I also wonder what the full extent of the toxic mould might have been and if Peddle has taken the proper steps to ensure the safety of future tenants after his remodel.

If you want to understand what "Rock Solid" seems to mean to Peddle, just read the following text exchange between Peddle and me and notice that in that exchange Peddle disavowed the ownership that he had previously proclaimed to law enforcement, to tenants, and to other governmental or quasi-governmental bodies, as well as denied any responsibility for his actions.

I guess Peddle only wanted to claim ownership when it suited his purposes to do so or when he believed it made him look important, but once it became inconvenient, he just wanted to wash his hands of it, as he did with his former tenants. I still don't know for sure whether the lie was that he was an owner, or whether the lie was that he wasn't an owner. I just know both cannot be true.

I am disgusted by these types of slum landlords who use the underprivileged and disenfranchised as pawns in their efforts to make a few dollars. Now you know how Peddle and Peddle Construction have earned a few pages in my book.

ME 11/22/13 9:56 AM

. . . . .It's not just on the street that your word has to have meaning, it's in business too. I know; I've owned several companies far more successful than yours. It's about "honor" and "integrity," about doing "the right thing," about a "just outcome" and about "what you are," not "who you think you should be." On the street, as in business, you get one chance to earn "respect" and a thousand chances to blow it; you have done nothing but blow it so far. There are people at Douglas Manor still. It's time for you to quit blowing it and finally "man up" and do "the right thing" by them and by yourself, and just maybe begin earning their respect and your own self respect in the process. It could change Christmas for all of you and maybe forever change your future and that of your family. I'm watching from a not too distant perch. I've been watching.

PEDDLE CONSTRUCTION 11/22/13 10:08 AM

Thanks for the threat._I have nothing to do with that building. I was a contractor who was supposed to Reno but as you can see, never happened. Contact the owners if you have a problem

ME 11/22/13 10:11 AM

I have no problem and there was no threat, but as far as just being a contractor who was supposed to do renos goes, that is not how you represented yourself to the VicPD or the RTB, so the friendly advice still holds. Good luck to you.

PEDDLE CONSTRUCTION 11/22/13 10:13 AM

Don't contact me anymore

I sent Peddle a text telling him of my intended publication of this book and letting him know that he had earned mention in it because of his lies. In that text, I invited Peddle to add his comments. Peddle never responded.

The message here is that if you have trouble with those of Peddle's ilk on your journey through the rental market, contact me and I will put you in touch with those who can assist you, or I will try to assist you myself in any manner in which the law allows me to be involved. Just be aware that all legal notices from landlords come with time deadlines and that you must comply with those deadlines.

Peddle may have gotten one thing right though when he said, "He may be sixty-six, but he's like no sixty-six year old you have ever met." Most people will not include you in their book just to set the record straight. I'm still laughing.

END OF BOOK QUESTIONS

23. Did this book make you think about your principles and values?
24. Did you find the quotes at the beginning of each chapter helpful in understanding the content of that chapter?
25. Did this book change the way you think about drugs?
26. Did this book educate you about why most drug addicts turned to drugs in the first place?
27. Do you think that you can try drugs and not get addicted?
28. Are you going to talk to your family about drugs now?
29. Did this book show you results of child abuse about which you never thought?
30. Did this change the way you think about abuse of women?
31. Did this book help you better understand the pressures on our youth?
32. Did this book give you a deeper appreciation for the police?
33. Did this book make you want to get involved in helping any of the many categories of people who are part of it?
34. Do you think that you should now feel sorry for most drug addicts, rather than scornful?

Post your answers on www.breakingthecode.ca.

Although any information that might be used to identify you will remain absolutely confidential, some of the data gathered from your answers might be compiled and shown to politicians, news media and/or other organizations that may benefit from your opinions.

If you enjoyed this book or think it might help anybody you know, please scroll to the next page and tell your social media friends about it.

Finally, I invite you to like us on Facebook and to post a review of this book on www.breakingthecode.ca .

Thank you for taking time to go online and to answer the questions, and thank you for reading Breaking the Code.

Made in the USA
Charleston, SC
08 December 2014